Changing Pastors

A RESOURCE FOR PASTORAL TRANSITIONS

Changing Pastors

A RESOURCE FOR PASTORAL TRANSITIONS

Thomas P. Sweetser, S.J.
Mary Benet McKinney, O.S.B.

Sheed & Ward
Kansas City

Sheed & Ward™ is a service of National Catholic Reporter Publishing Company, Inc.

Library of Congress Cataloging-in-Publication Data.
Sweetser, Thomas P.
    Changing pastors : a resource for pastoral transitions / Thomas P. Sweetser, Mary Benet McKinney.
        p. cm.
    Includes bibliographical references and index.
    ISBN: 1-55612-961-0 (alk. paper)
    1. Catholic Church—Clergy—Relocation. 2. Catholic Church—Clergy—Appointment, call, and election. I. McKinney, Mary Benet. II. Title.
BX1912.S795   1998
254—dc21   97-48834
                                                           CIP

Published by: Sheed & Ward
              115 E. Armour Blvd.,
              P.O. Box 419492
              Kansas City, MO 64141-6492.

To order, call: (800)333-7373

This book is printed on recycled paper.

Cover design by Emil Antonucci.

www.natcath.com/sheedward

Contents

Acknowledgments iv

Foreword v

Chapter One
Give Transition Its Due 1

Chapter Two
Transition as a Way of Life 6

Chapter Three
Gathering the Ingredients Together 20

Chapter Four
Preparing to Say Good-bye 35

Chapter Five
The Chaos and Creativity of the Interim 78

Chapter Six
May I Have This Dance? 101

Chapter Seven
Could We Do This on Our Own? 131

Chapter Eight
Wisdom for the Journey 160

Bibliography
Times of Transition 177

Transition Process 179

ACKNOWLEDGMENTS

This book was the work of many wise and generous people, primarily those who participated in the original project involving three dioceses. We wish to thank the diocesan committee members, the outgoing and prospective pastors involved in the process and especially the many parishioners who made up the parish transition teams. This last group contributed life and energy to the process by their humor, dedication and fresh insight. Others helped in the final stages of the book who we would like to name individually. These include Mary Borowicz, Kathleen and Richard Hage, James Fanelli and John Reid. We dedicate this work to the parish of the twenty-first century, hoping that the transition process we offer may help it thrive and become a reflection of God's love in the world.

FOREWORD

"Life is change. Change is growth. Growth is painful." These words, spoken by my mom on countless occasions to her seven children provide an important challenge to all readers of this new, important and much needed book. *Changing Pastors: A Resource for Pastoral Transitions* is a gold mine of hard-won insight and wisdom on the challenges and opportunities provided by times of change and transition. Mary Benet McKinney and Tom Sweetser rightly identify times of pastoral transition as key moments for leaders and communities to work together and find new life, to grow stronger rather than become disconnected.

Do you believe that "life is change"? If you agree with my mom that this is true, then this book will provide you the opportunity to reflect on what you can do to work with the changes that come into your life. Tom and Mary Benet do focus on the parish setting and the challenges of pastoral transition. Readers will learn much that applies to this occasional reality. At the same time, insights from this book apply to many other situations in which we face change.

Do you believe that "change is growth"? I believe this is sometimes the case. Times of change can be times of growth, but this is not necessarily so. Some people experience change that is damaging or debilitating. Mary Benet and Tom recognize this reality and present ways individuals and communities can deal with change so that growth and new life is more likely. This professional and personal resource provides guidelines, tested by experience, that give the reader specific, practical ways of moving through the change experience that will also promote growth. Their examples, stories and handouts provide a true resource for use by readers.

Do you believe that "growth is painful"? I do, because all growth involves some letting go or loss in order to embrace the new. New life, for individuals and communities, requires movement from what is ending through an uncertain or in-between time to a new life or new beginning. *Changing Pastors* introduces the reader to a process for making this important movement. Yes, there is pain, but there can be joy as well, for this journey from one stage to another is also our journey of faith, from death into new life. While changes happen within any organization, people of faith have a crucial resource to use during times of change. Mary Benet and Tom weave the Christian faith story through this book in their times of prayer and in reflections on the various stages in the process of transition.

I began coordinating Transition Services within the Catholic Archdiocese of Seattle in 1989. For the past nine years I have worked with pastors and communities in transition. I can testify from personal experience that times of pastoral change are indeed times of crisis for our leaders and communities of faith. In fact, the Chinese word for "crisis" is made up of two characters that mean "danger" and "opportunity." I believe Tom and Mary Benet provide us a blueprint for how individuals, dioceses and faith communities can recognize the dangers and maximize the opportunities for growth.

The Spirit is alive and well, calling leaders and communities to new life amidst the challenge and chaos of change. I commend this wonderful new resource to all who desire to grow stronger in the midst of change and transition. To paraphrase my mom, life is change, change can be growthful and growth is both painful and joyful. Thank you Mary Benet and Tom, for showing us the way through times of change to growth, joy and new life.

John M. Reid

Chapter One

Give Transition Its Due

St. Mary's was a thriving parish. People flocked to its liturgies. Each Mass had its own flavor and clientele. There were organizations and groups for every age and area of interest. The staff worked well together and enjoyed each other's company. A spirit of accomplishment pervaded the council and commissions.

When asked what was the reason for this success, people pointed to the pastor as the cause. During the twelve years of his tenure he had slowly but surely coaxed and cajoled the parish community to take ownership of the parish, to share gifts and talents, wisdom and insight, to reveal the Spirit at work in their midst.

That was last year. Times have changed. In July, the pastor's term of office came to an end. He was replaced by a well-meaning, spiritual priest who had limited vision and not much self-confidence. He had no idea what he had taken on or how to cope with the energy, creativity and ownership of the parish community.

The laughter and joy of the staff diminished. The council meetings became labored. The Masses lacked energy. The teens became despondent and the parish slowly returned to the mediocre, uneventful church it had been years before. The parishioners did not complain. The new pastor was well-meaning, but he didn't have the capacity to lead a vibrant parish. Middle-of-the-road was his style and people became accustomed to not expecting much from his leadership. Some parishioners left the parish in search of a more vital community. Others decided to wait him out in hopes that he might change or that he would be transferred a few years hence, though they knew this would be unlikely.

Did this have to happen? Is there another story that could have been told about St. Mary's? We feel there is. What was missing in this story is a process of transition that would have taken into account the history and climate of the parish, one that paid attention to the people's needs and expectations, as well as to the gifts and abilities of the new pastor. A tragedy in the American Catholic Church is that precious little time, energy and even less money are spent on the period of transition when there is a change of pastors. Had St. Mary's had the benefit of a year-long transition process, this crisis in leadership may not have occurred.

We would like to think that the role of pastor is not as dominant as it was before the Second Vatican Council when the parish "belonged" to the pastor, someone who was often appointed for life. The impact of the pastor should lessen with the new emphasis on shared leadership and collaborative ministry. Not so. The style and tone may have changed, but the influence is still just as great. We know this from personal experience with many "St. Mary's" across the country. Parishes undergo profound shifts with the change of pastors. The change demands careful attention and concerted effort so that neither the parish nor the incoming pastor is destroyed in the process.

This is what we have tried to do in a few dioceses and what we offer in this book as an alternative model for the placement of pastors in parishes. Our motto is: "Give transition the attention it deserves." The focus is not just on the pastor who is leaving or the one who is coming in to replace him. Rather, it takes into account the diocesan system of replacement as well as the parish community undergoing the change.

Over the last year, we have tested this process in three dioceses and have received assurances that it is a better way of proceeding than what happened at St. Mary's, where one pastor followed on the heels of another, with neither the priests nor the people being adequately consulted or prepared for the shift.

The process begins on the diocesan level with a commitment to giving the transition of pastors extra time and special attention. At the outset, both the priests and the parishes of the diocese are informed about this new approach to transition. A special transition committee is formed that is made up of people who have the time to devote to this important ministry and that has a budget equal to the task.

The priests and the people of the diocese are not only informed about the transition process but are given the opportunity to discuss this approach and to voice their reactions, fears and concerns. This dialogue is an essential ingredient for the process to succeed, especially among the clergy. One of the learning experiences we had in testing out the model in the three dioceses is that not enough information was disseminated in the diocese nor was there adequate discussion about it among the priests. As a result, some pastors, when approached about participating in the project, were apprehensive because they did not know enough about it or what it entailed. Dialogue is important, but so is commitment, especially by the local ordinary, the diocesan personnel board and the chancery staff. The mindset that makes this transition process work is that they realize the placement of pastors in parishes is the key to their success as diocesan resource people. It is our experience that there is a better chance that the time and energy spent during the transition process will be rewarded with a happy parish community and a contented, fulfilled pastor. Not paying attention to this change in pastors can lead to frustrated clergy and disheartened people, which adds to the workload of diocesan personnel as they try to deal with parish conflicts.

Had St. Mary's parish been part of such a process, the present tone would be different. What we offer in this book is a process that we know works. We have experienced its success in three pilot dioceses. It works best when it is done with a group of parishes, ideally three to six at a time. It can also be done within a single parish, although the shared insights, companionship and support of groups of pastors and parish leaders is lost.

Life is never perfect. If there is one thing we have learned in testing the process, it is the need to be flexible. Priests and parishes do not fit into prearranged, patterned molds. Each has a unique story to tell, a special set of circumstances, a personal set of needs and timelines to follow. One size does not fit all.

What we offer in the following chapters is a general framework for transition that can be adapted to fit each situation. It is presented as a model for the change of pastors involving a group of parishes. The model can also be applied to other types of transitions, either on a personal level or those involving a group or organization. It can be adapted for changes involving other staff positions besides the pastor, or for changes in religious congregations, school principals or chancery staff.

One possible application is the placement of a new bishop in a diocese. What a spiritual awakening could go on among Catholics if they were invited into a year-long process of reflection and discernment as to what makes their diocese unique and what type of bishop would be needed to give it direction. Rather than just a few people being consulted in private about a new bishop, the ideas and insights of many could contribute much to the process.

The outgoing bishop would also have the opportunity to let go of the position with grace and forethought. The fact that little happens now on a diocesan level is no reason that it could not or should not have the attention paid to it in the future. Hopefully, a change in the placement process on the parish level will affect the diocesan level as well.

The bishop in one of our pilot dioceses shared his story of the transition process he experienced when he was appointed bishop. It reveals how little time and attention is provided to those who take on this assignment. He told of learning about his appointment in a brief conversation with his superior during a break at a bishop's meeting. He could not share the news with anyone, nor could he adequately prepare for the new situation. He did not find the adjustment easy, although he could not share his feelings with anyone in the diocese for fear that they would think there was something wrong with them or with the diocese. Thus he was never given time to grieve the loss of his previous ministry nor was he provided with an interim period to prepare for his new job. In order to prevent this from happening in our Church, we submit the following process as a more grace-filled way of undergoing transitions, especially in the change of pastors.

Chapter Two

Transition as a Way of Life

Transitions are the stuff of life. Some are sudden, others occur over long periods of time. Some are planned for and others surprise us. Some are happy occasions and some are painful. One element of transition remains constant. They are all traumatic experiences that grab our attention and use up large amounts of our time and energy.

A young couple is expecting a new baby. It is their first child. They have a number of months to plan for the arrival. When it comes, however, the routine of their lives is severely changed and shaken.

A woman goes to the doctor complaining of a cough that won't go away only to discover she has lung cancer. Subsequent operations and chemotherapy are successful so that the cancer is no longer life-threatening. The memory of the experience remains. Her life is forever changed.

Even the comparatively gentle transitions, such as a change in homes or jobs, can be so disruptive as to cause sleep loss, anxiety and irritableness that continue for some time after the change has taken place.

Transitions in Scripture

The Bible is filled with transitions and how people are changed in the process. The stories of Adam and Eve, Noah, Abraham and Sarah, Ruth, Moses, David are all accounts of transitions from one situation to another and what effects they had on the key players and on those around them.

Three important moments of transition occur in the Gospels. One is the moment Jesus decides to leave his home and travel to the Jordan to investigate his cousin John's actions. Jesus felt drawn to a baptism of commitment and from there is led into the desert. This is an interim period during which he prepares for his new life. Temptations are common in this in-between stage. "What am I doing here? Why did I agree to do this? What did I commit to? What is going to happen to me? Am I up to this?" These are all very real questions in the chaotic period between what was left behind and what lies ahead. Jesus comes through the test and sets his whole being toward fulfilling "my Father's will."

A second example of transition is the "feast of Holy Saturday." This is a forgotten feast on the Church's calendar. The followers of Jesus had just experienced a devastating blow to their faith and hope in Jesus. They saw him die. It appeared that he was gone forever. Life would never be the same. Despair and depression settled in during the in-between time of Holy Saturday. Had Jesus reappeared immediately after his death, this important period of grieving, coping with the loss, reflecting on what had been and what he meant to his followers, would have been lost. These few days of confusion and anxiety prepared the way for the acceptance of the risen Christ. The women learned this lesson well. They encountered the new reality and shared it with the apostles, but to no avail. Transition takes time. We have to be able to embrace the change and be open to a new way of life and existence. It took the disciples a long time, at least forty days, to catch on.

The third transitional moment was the interim between the Ascension and Pentecost. This may have been one of the most difficult periods of transition for Jesus. He had to leave his little flock or they would have remained dependent on him and never would have assumed responsibility for spreading the Good News. But as he left them, he must have asked himself, "Is this group of motley characters going to keep this thing alive?"

He does leave and the disciples are left looking up into a cloud. They are instructed to return to their familiar place and wait. For what, they were not sure. This is a classic period of "in-between time," an important step in letting go of what was and getting ready for what will be. By the time the Spirit comes and shakes their foundations, they are ready. They are able to open themselves to their new task of spreading the word. This little band of frightened followers becomes a confident group of evangelizers, speaking to people's hearts in words they can understand.

The Stages of Transition

> What we call the beginning is often the end
> And to make an end is to make a beginning.
> The end is where we start from.
>
> > T. S. Eliot
> > "Little Gidding" (1942)

William Bridges, in his groundbreaking work on transition (*Transitions: Making Sense of Life Changes* and *Managing Transitions*), identifies three stages associated with every transition. First comes the *ending* stage. This is the period before a change takes place. It has various lengths, even for the people undergoing the same transitional experience. In a given parish, the pastor may begin thinking about a change more than a year in advance of his move. Some staff members may learn of the shift only a few months before his departure. Many of the less active parishioners first learn about the change when they hear it from the pastor himself the final weekend he is in the parish.

Whether of long or short duration, this stage of *endings* is filled with many conflicting emotions and behaviors, including disorganization, disengagement, letting go and withdrawal. The pastor may feel sad he is leaving but glad to be putting some of the difficult aspects of leading the parish behind him. The staff members may become disorganized in their work as they try to plan for an uncertain future. Parishioners struggle to put closure to the pastor's leadership while trying to come to grips with the fact that the pastor is indeed leaving.

The second stage is the *neutral zone* or the *in-between time*. This period overlaps with the first because both pastor and people, in preparing for the transition, feel as if they are in limbo. They are uncertain, anxious, confused, unbelieving, at a loss. As the termination rituals for the departing pastor take place, the staff, leaders and people are left wondering "what's next?"

It is this *in-between time* that is not acknowledged or given its due in the typical method for a change of pastors in American Catholic parishes. In most cases, as soon as one pastor leaves, another arrives. This approach allows for no time in which the people can mourn the loss of one leader and open their hearts to another.

What is lost in this rapid succession of pastors is the chance for creative reflection by both leaders and people about who they are as a parish, what is unique and special about them, no matter who the pastor may be. This is the most traumatic time for a parish. People want security. They want to know who will be their new pastor. While this neutral period of unknowing and uncertainty can be creative, it is also chaotic.

Eventually a new pastor does arrive, but the *in-between* stage continues for some time as people begin to discover the "tone" of the new pastorate. If it is a good match, then anxieties and apprehensions diminish and acceptance grows. If the transition was not well-planned and prepared for, or if there was no interval between the outgoing and incoming pastor, then the *in-between* stage lasts much longer. Many new pastors have experienced a long period of "settling in" because people have not had a chance to grieve the loss of the former pastor. There is little room in their hearts to welcome the new pastor, so the neutral phase lasts longer than is necessary or healthy for a parish community.

The *in-between* stage blends into the third stage of *new beginnings*. As the new pastor assumes leadership, uncertainty gives way to a new way of being parish. People make comparisons with how he differs from the previous pastor, what is unique in his approach and emphasis, how he is similar and how he is different. The transition comes to an end as the period of *new beginnings* becomes familiar to the pastor, the leaders and the people. Usually this new way of operating becomes predictable in six months to a year. Everyone settles into "this is the way we do things around here." Those who are attracted by and agree with the new style come forward with their support and affirmation. Those who find it not to their liking withdraw, learn to live with the situation or "wait it out" until the next transition takes place.

This is the William Bridges understanding of the stages of transition. A second interpretation comes from a book by Sabina Spencer and John Adams called *Life Changes*. In working with groups that are undergoing a change in leadership, this explanation of transition proved most helpful and supportive.

Moving Through Transitions

Spencer and Adams describe seven stages of transition. Figure A shows the dynamics that people who are experiencing transition go through.

Figure A
Stages of Transition

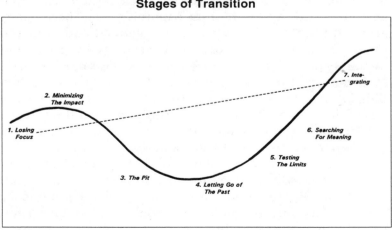

Source: Sabrina Spencer and John Adams,
Life Changes (Impact Publishers, 1990)

Consider a pastor who loves the parish but decides that it will soon be time to move to another. When he first confronts the reality that he may actually be moving on, he experiences an initial loss of clarity and focus, even in his everyday chores and priestly duties. "Am I really serious about this?" he asks. As he mulls over his decision, he becomes distracted and lost in thought. He is not concentrating and people notice an absentmindedness.

This loss of focus passes as he comes to the realization that "yes, this really will be my final year here." He begins settling into the next stage of trying to "minimize the impact" of his decision. Now that he knows that he is leaving, he tries to act as if all were normal. He goes about his regular tasks as usual. He expects to sail right through the transition to the final stage of integration into the new parish, with no problems, regrets or misgivings. He would like to move up the dotted line and never experience the pitfalls of transition. This never happens. Much as we strive to make transitions smooth and without incident, they always include uncertainty, anxiety and trauma.

Without realizing it, the pastor begins to slide into the "pit of transition." Even our pleasant, desirable transitions have a "pit" stage associated with them. "Why did I decide to do this?" the pastor begins to ask. "This is going to be really hard. Too many good friends, too many great moments, too many unrealized dreams are part of this place. Maybe I should stay a few more years."

Much as he would like to, he can no longer go back to the place he was before his decision. Much as he tries to avoid it, there is nothing ahead that looks as appealing as what he now has. He is in the pit with feelings of depression, anger, loss, sadness, ambiguity and rootlessness. The staff and parishioners notice the difference and ask if he is feeling all right.

This pit stage of transition can be of long or short duration, but it cannot be avoided. Then one morning the pastor wakes up with not quite as heavy a heart. He sees a little glimmer in the gloom. He is beginning to let go of his present pastorate and all it has meant to him. Very soon he falls back down into the pit, but for a brief moment there was some movement to the next stage of "letting go of the past." Slowly he moves further up out of the pit as he begins to say good-bye in his own heart to what he has enjoyed and held dear – his home, those aspects of pastoring he liked the most, the people who have been supportive and steadfast on his journey.

In letting go he starts making room for other thoughts that are more future oriented. "What will I do next? What will the next place be like? What new things should I try out? What unfulfilled ambitions do I have that might now be possible? What difficult aspects of my present job will I be able to leave behind?" Our pastor is beginning to "test out new limits" in his letting go. He experiences a freedom he did not have before. He is looking ahead instead of just looking back. The letting go is allowing him to think new thoughts, dream new dreams, vague and fleeting as these may be.

As he moves through the good-byes and the leave-taking, and as he takes time off before assuming new responsibilities, he will have a chance to reflect on his journey of transition and search for what it has meant to him. He begins to ask, "What new things did I learn about myself? What was hard and what was easy about it? What were the surprises and what was I able to predict? In what ways have I become more prayerful, more loving, more accepting, more patient? What compulsions and strengths did this move reveal?"

In searching for answers to these questions, the pastor begins to integrate the transition experience into his personality and worldview. Had he sailed through the transition without experiencing the pit, he would have lost all the self-knowledge and personal learning it afforded him.

The pit cannot be avoided. If the pastor does not deal with his feelings of loss, grief and withdrawal during the period of change, they will come later. The difficulty with putting it off is that he will have to deal with these feelings while adjusting to his new pastorate or retirement. Besides trying to cope with all the challenges this entails, he will also have to deal with unresolved loss and inadequate closure from the previous parish. All the more reason that pastors be given an extended period to deal with transition whenever they change jobs.

The pastor, however, is not the only one experiencing the pit during this transition. It affects the staff, parish leaders and people as well. Consider the feelings of the staff when he announces one day in January that he is thinking about asking for another assignment starting in the fall. It comes as a bombshell. He is loved, he is a team player, a facilitating leader, a visionary for the staff and the parish as a whole. They try to change his mind, talk him out of leaving, deny it is happening, grope for reasons why this should not take place.

The announcement results in a sudden loss of focus for the staff. Similar feelings are expressed by the council and the parish as a whole when the news begins to spread. But soon they recover. In trying to put the best "spin" on the announcement, they seek to minimize the impact the pastor's leaving will have on the parish. "We can do it. He's taught us to take initiative. He has empowered us to own the parish. No one can come in and destroy what we have built up in recent years."

Try as they might, the parish and its leadership begin to slide down into the pit. It is in a funk. "What will become of us? Why is he abandoning us like this? It will never be the same." No amount of reassurance or affirmation from the pastor has any effect. Tempers flare, conflicts arise, work slackens, people withdraw into themselves and into their own ministries. The pit experience is unavoidable. If, however, it is expected and prepared for, it need not debilitate the leaders or the people. They need to let go of the past as much as the pastor does. That is why, as we will explain in subsequent chapters, the leaders and the people need to gather to discuss what they are willing to let go of and what new things they may want to try out. This helps them test out new limits and directions for the parish, to seek new horizons and a new way of being parish.

This business of letting go and testing out new limits takes time. Part of it can happen while the outgoing pastor is still present. Some of it needs to happen after he has gone and before the new person has arrived. This is one reason for scheduling into the transition process an interim period between pastors. Even a short space of a few weeks to a month helps people let go of the old and look forward to the new. It is during this time that the leaders and people reflect on the transition and discover aspects about themselves and the parish they had never noticed before. "We *were* able to function without a pastor. We discovered new strengths and resources we didn't know we had. We are unique and special as a parish, irrespective of who our pastor may be." If this period of discovery can go on before the new pastor arrives, the parish is much better equipped to bond with the new person and to integrate the pastor into the life of the parish.

The scenario we have been describing thus far relates to a parish where the outgoing pastor is well-liked and cherished as a friend and gifted leader. What if the opposite is true? The pastor who is leaving is not popular. The announcement of his leaving comes more as a relief than a sorrow.

This situation, perhaps more so than the previous example, needs time for saying good-byes and for allowing memories to heal, both by the pastor and the people. It also needs an interim period between pastors so that staff, leaders and parishioners can catch their breath, think positively about the change and prepare themselves for the new person. The pastor, more than anyone, needs time to reflect on the experience, learn from his mistakes, assess his gifts and strong points and head into his new assignment with new energy and a positive spirit. In this case, an extended interim period, perhaps even a six-month or yearlong sabbatical would be most beneficial. It would give the outgoing pastor time for updating, spiritual renewal and physical rejuvenation. Time spent in this in-between stage will reap many rewards for the pastor himself, and for the parishioners in his new assignment.

What about the incoming pastor? Not only is the outgoing pastor and the parish undergoing change, so is the new pastor. Whether the person is a priest, a deacon or a nonordained pastoral administrator, he or she is also going through the same stages of transition. What traumatic experiences of transition has the new pastor been facing in leaving the previous assignment? What sadness or loss lies in this person's heart? Has he or she had a chance to have an interim period between jobs, time to let go, to recoup and prepare for the new ministry? The parish is waiting, perhaps with anticipation, anxiety and uncertainty, for the new pastor. Is the new person ready for all these mixed and varied emotions?

One pastor described a single day in his life that he said he never wants to repeat. He began the Sunday by presiding at his final three Masses at a parish he dearly loved and that loved him. All smiles and laughter he said one final good-bye at a reception following the Masses. He then got into his car piled high with what was left of his moving and drove to his new parish, tears streaming down his face. He arrived in the afternoon at an empty rectory. There was no sign of welcoming, no food in the refrigerator, no acknowledgment of his coming. It took him many months to recover from this experience. In fairness to the parishioners, they were given the wrong date for his arrival, but that did not take away his "pit" experience. It should never be like this. What we offer in the following pages is another model for the transition of pastors, one that is more healthy and growthful for all concerned.

The Process of Transition

Many Protestant denominations understand the importance of the transition period between pastors. They spend a great deal of time and effort trying to help both the pastors and the parishes through the transition. Few Catholic dioceses give to this period of flux the attention it merits. We have also become aware that more than just the priests are affected by the change. The staff, leaders and people are critically affected as well.

With this in mind, we proposed a model of transition as a pilot project to three dioceses of varying sizes and complexity. The process we used included four groups and had three phases that began in September of one year and ended in November of the following year.

The four groups we worked with in each diocese included a diocesan committee that acted as the oversight group and the coordinators of the process. Members of the committee acted as contacts to each of the pastors and parishes involved in transition. A second group was the outgoing pastors who would be leaving their parishes sometime between May and July. The third group was a collection of transition teams, one from each parish that was undergoing a change of pastors. The fourth group included all the priests and pastoral administrators who were interested in becoming pastors in the soon-to-be-open parishes.

In September, each of the three target dioceses assembled a committee that included members of the priests' personnel board and those involved in the placement of nonordained parish administrators. The diocesan committees ranged in size from six to ten members. At an initial meeting with the diocesan committee, we laid out the process we would follow and clarified their roles and duties.

Their first duty was to contact the pastors who would be moving the next summer to elicit their support and involvement. These pastors were asked to select a transition team in their parish that would shepherd the parish through the transition process. Both the outgoing pastors and the transition teams were asked to attend a workshop during the month of January.

All the pastors who would be leaving their parish sometime during the summer months gathered for a one-day workshop in January. The focus of the gathering was to explain the process of transition, to help them reflect on their pastorate and to help them put closure to their term as pastor.

The transition teams gathered for two evening meetings during the same week as the pastors' workshop. It was here that they learned about their role as overseers of the transition in the parish. It was their task to facilitate meetings with the staff and lay leaders that would help the leadership deal with the transition. The team would also hold a series of town hall meetings for parishioners. The purpose of the town halls was to gather information about what the people wanted to hold on to, what they were willing to let go of, and what new things they would like to try out when the new pastor arrived.

These meetings of leadership and parishioners would lead to a report that the parish transition team would submit to the diocese. The report would contain information about what made the parish unique, what qualities the new pastor would need for leading the parish and what issues or challenges a new pastor might be facing.

During the same period, a half-day workshop was held for prospective pastors and pastoral administrators as a way of tying them into the process. This gave them a chance to begin thinking about the parishes that would be vacant in the summer and whether they would like to apply to be pastors in any of these parishes. It also helped them to reflect on their own vision of parish and style of leadership and to identify what was negotiable and what was not negotiable as they began to prepare for a new assignment.

The months between January and June were filled with activity. The outgoing pastors were putting their homes and offices in order, saying their good-byes, preparing a new place for themselves and helping the parish make room for the new pastor.

The transition teams were gathering leaders and people together for input and reflection about the parish, all of which led to a brief report on the life and style, the needs and strengths of the parish. These reports were finished in April and hand delivered to the contact person from the diocesan transition committee. In May the prospective pastors had the reports in hand and were beginning to make decisions about which places they might like to apply for. Some prospective pastors even visited the open parishes to put flesh on the written reports. There was never any expectation, however, that the prospective pastors were being "interviewed" by the parish leadership or transition team. The placement was in the hands of the bishop and personnel board. What this period of study and reflection provided was a better sense of what the parish was like, what it could offer or might demand of the new pastor. This information helped the prospective pastors make a more informed judgment about whether they should apply as a possible candidate for the parish. The prospective pastors made their requests and the diocese named the new pastors sometime between May and July.

Another set of workshops was held during the "in-between time" of June and July. By June the outgoing pastors either had left their parishes or were close to leaving. They came together for a morning of reflection on their experience of transition as they began looking ahead to their next assignment and new home. The transition teams met for two evenings to share their experiences of writing the parish reports and of helping the pastor say good-bye. This was a traumatic time for the parishioners as they tried to cope with the interim period between one pastor and the next. The predominant feelings were insecurity and ambivalence because they were left without a leader and were uncertain what the new person might bring to the parish.

The prospective pastors' workshop was in two parts. The morning was for all those who came to the initial session in January. Only some of these people would become pastors in the vacant parishes. This was a time to share stories of what they would be leaving, what lay ahead, what were their disappointments and joys, what were areas of growth and new learning. The afternoon session was for those who had been assigned to new parishes. It was geared toward specifics about each new place and what the new pastors were planning to do and what they would be facing. They were encouraged to take a break between assignments so they could let go of the old and get ready for the new.

Sometime during July and August the new assignments took effect and the new pastors moved in. Over September and October the new pastors and parishes went through the welcoming rituals and started to become acquainted with each other.

In October and November a final set of workshops was held for the transition teams and the new pastors. The first workshop was an evening for the transition teams at which they shared with each other a timeline of the last four months of transition. The next day the new pastors gathered together to tell stories of how they were welcomed and integrated into the parish. Finally, the two groups came together for a common meal and an evening of sharing. The transition teams and the new pastors compared timelines noting the emphases and highlights of each. They also shared ideas about what lay ahead for the parish and what new directions it might take. This became the culminating event in the transition process. The transition teams had done their task and could now return to their regular routine in the parish. The new pastors had a much better sense of what they would be facing in the months and years ahead. They also had people they could count on for honest feedback and genuine support.

Each diocese had its own time frame and way of progressing through the steps of transition. The pilot project taught us above all about the need to be flexible. Nothing worked out exactly as planned. What we offer in this book is a general framework that can be adapted and changed to fit each unique situation. In the next four chapters we will spell out in detail the various stages in the yearlong transition process, along with stories and anecdotes from those who took part in the process.

Following those chapters are two others that spell out how this approach can be used for other individuals and groups that are going through pastoral transitions. We conclude with recommendations and insights based upon our experience with the three dioceses and the twelve parishes involved in the project. At the end of each chapter, we include prayer services and handout materials that we have developed during the project. We are available for on-site consultation with dioceses, parishes or other groups who desire facilitation and guidance through the process of transition.

Chapter Three

Gathering the Ingredients Together

Concern for good leadership in the Church began with Jesus and his call and missioning of the first apostles. Paul in his letter to Titus puts it this way:

> For this reason I left you in Crete so that you might set right what remains to be done and appoint presbyters in every town, as I directed you, on condition that . . . as God's stewards (they) must be blameless, not arrogant, not irritable, not drunkards, not aggressive, not greedy for sordid gain, but hospitable, lovers of goodness, temperate, just, holy and self-controlled, holding fast to the true message as taught so that they will be able to both exhort with sound doctrine and refute opponents.
>
> (Titus 1:5-9)

That degree of concern continues to exist today. Three things were clear as we began working with each of the three dioceses:

- The placement of pastors is a critical issue.

- Although changes have been made in the process, the methods currently used are inadequate and often ineffective.

- Bishops and those who work with them in personnel offices recognize the need for a better system.

Selling the pilot, in other words, was not that difficult. The challenge was to gather a diocesan transition committee of people who had sufficient commitment to the project to give it the time and energy needed to shepherd the process through its many stages. They also needed enough conviction and stamina to keep pushing against the current placement system with all its expectations. This diocesan transition committee had to be the glue that would hold the process together, the spark that would keep it moving forward and the guide that would keep it on track.

The single greatest weakness of the three committees was that every member was asked to add this task to an already full plate of responsibilities. It was our recommendation, and theirs as well, to name a project director to name who would be able to give significant time to the transition process. The other committee members also had to be freed from some of their other responsibilities if the transition committee was going to be effective in providing the guidance, the support and the presence demanded by the parish transition teams and the pastors.

Having said that, we hasten to add that we marveled at the work done by the three diocesan transition committees. They were responsible for much of the success of the pilot and made every effort to live up to their tasks and obligations.

The role played by the local bishop became clearer to us as we worked through the project. The size of the diocese and the leadership style of the bishop had to be taken into account. But the success of the project was directly related to the involvement, or at least the commitment, of the bishop. Both the clergy and the diocesan transition committee needed the encouragement and support of the local ordinary. To assume this was not enough. The bishop needed to be visibly connected to the project. What he said to the presbyterate would go a long way in freeing the clergy to embrace this new approach.

The Role of the Diocesan Transition Committee

The work of the diocesan committee was to motivate, lead, organize, guide and evaluate all facets of the project. Its **tasks** included:

1. Initial contact and ongoing communication with all groups associated with the transition process.

2. Calling forth and encouraging the participation of clergy and parishes of the diocese in this new approach to the placement of pastors.

3. Identifying pastors and parishes who are undergoing transition.

4. Establishing timelines and schedules for the process.

5. Planning and facilitating workshops for outgoing pastors, parish transition teams, pastoral staffs and potential pastors.

6. Attending workshops and committee meetings throughout the process.

7. Accepting responsibility to act as liaison to one of the parishes undergoing change.

8. Evaluating the process at each stage of the transition.

9. Formulating recommendations for adjustments in succeeding years.

Membership on the diocesan committee was determined by interest, commitment, skill and experience. People considered for the task included members of priests' personnel boards, members of diocesan lay ministry training and pastoral council offices, as well as those connected to non-ordained placement and pastoral planning. Skills included written and verbal proficiency, group process, listening skills, tolerance, adaptability and proficiency in public relations.

Some of the expectations for membership on the committee included:

• Attendance at all committee meetings.

- Sharing in the responsibility for planning and facilitating the workshops.
- Accepting responsibility for an individual parish, which included:

  1. Assisting the parish transition team as needed.

  2. Attending parish town hall meetings.

  3. Receiving the parish report and profile from the transition teams and passing it on to the personnel board.

  4. Maintaining regular communication with the pastor and parish team.

One of the frustrations we faced in all three dioceses was a lack of uniform practice regarding a pastor's departure from a parish. This was complicated by an unhealthy tradition of secrecy. It did not appear acceptable for a pastor to announce to the parish six months or a year in advance that he was leaving the parish. The process was hampered by attitudes of secrecy and unclear diocesan structures. People seeking pastorates did not know which parishes would be available and when. Parishes were left guessing about their future rather than planning ahead for it. Rumors and speculation were grist for the ecclesial mill. A diocesan guideline giving a timetable for announcing resignations and allowing for sufficient time between the announcement and the actual leave-taking would be most helpful. It is our recommendation that dioceses develop a timeline that starts with the announcement of the pastor's leaving in December and ends with his actual departure the end of May. This would allows an interim between pastors during the month of June. At this time, the new pastor is named. He moves into the parish sometime during July or August.

One aspect of the transition process that was threatening to those involved in the pilot was the interim period. This is the time when the former pastor has left and the new person has not yet moved in. It is a "time-out period" for the leaders and people to catch their collective breath, let go of the pastor they have known and look forward to a new way of being parish. When we explained this part of the process to the priests and transition teams, it was initially either feared or rejected. In those parishes where the interim took place, however, it was recognized as a valuable time of growth for both the pastor and the parish. Despite the temptation to disregard the interim phase and have one pastor follow closely on the heels of another, we strongly recommend resisting the pressure to do this. Give it time. Let the ground lie fallow. Don't rush in to fill the vacuum of pastoral leadership.

One area that must be clearly spelled out and understood by all is the relationship of the diocesan transition committee to the outside facilitators of the process, as well as the role of these facilitators. The process of transition can be greatly enhanced if people from outside the diocesan system are utilized as facilitators throughout the process. This was our role in the pilot project. We saw ourselves as the trainers of the process, the ones who would work directly with the pastors and the parish transition teams to train them for their specific roles. It was also our expectation that the diocesan committee would work closely with us, thus learning how to become the facilitators of the process in the future.

While we worked directly with the pastors and parish transition teams, it was our expectation that a member of the diocesan committee would work closely with each individual parish. The balance was not always easy to maintain. The committee member was there to support, assist and challenge but not to do the work of the parish transition team. When the transition team worked smoothly, this presence and balance was established.

The other important relationship between the outside facilitators and the diocesan committee was one of ongoing communication. The more we knew about what was going on locally, the more helpful we could be to all those involved in the project.

Getting Started

Once a pastor agrees to be a part of the transition process, someone from the diocesan transition committee discusses with him what his responsibilities will be. Forming a parish transition committee is key among these responsibilities. We suggest that the committee include seven to twelve people.

Suggested Composition:

1. One staff member (not the pastor)

2. One council member (not the chairperson)

3. Two or three persons active in parish ministries or committees

4. One or two persons who have experienced previous parish transitions

5. Two members from the parish community who are not involved in leadership

Requisite skills for Transition Team members:

1. The ability to work well with groups

2. Good listening skills

3. The ability to synthesize large amounts of information

4. Skill in leading groups

5. The ability to motivate others

6. Ease in talking in front of groups

7. The ability to deal with conflict

8. Skills in being flexible and noncontrolling

The make-up of the transition team should include:

1. A balance of both men and women, as well as a variety of age groups

2. A variety of backgrounds that reflect the makeup of the parish

3. People who are accepted and credible in the parish community

4. People who are willing to attend the three diocesan workshops in January, June and October

5. People who are willing to commit themselves to the eleven-month process

6. People who will gather information and construct a parish report and profile

7. People who are open to ongoing training throughout the process

Just as the diocesan transition committee was the glue, the spark and the guide of the overall process, the individual parish transition teams fulfilled the same role locally. These teams varied in size from seven to twelve members. Our original design called for the outgoing pastor to appoint this team. As we will point out in the final chapter, the teams themselves recognized that they would have enjoyed greater credibility if their appointments had come from a joint decision of the outgoing pastor and the pastoral council. This would also have provided a greater sense of ownership and inclusion in the project by the pastoral council.

The parish transition teams were asked to participate in three training workshops of two evenings each. In each diocese, these sessions were held in a central location and brought together teams from all the parishes undergoing transition. Although this required extended travel time for some, the value of teams interacting with each other outweighed the inconvenience involved.

During the first phase of the project, the parish transition teams were asked to work with the outgoing pastor to helped him in his efforts to say good-bye in a graced and growthful way. The teams, along with other parish leaders, helped plan the farewell rituals and celebrations. They were encouraged to call the parishioners to appropriate expressions of gratitude for the pastor's years of service in the parish. For example, one team placed an open, empty suitcase in the sanctuary and invited the parishioners to write to the pastor, telling him how he had gifted them during his years of pastoring and place the letters in the suitcase.

The transition team was also required to gather data from the leaders and the parishioners that would eventually be the basis for a parish report and profile. The information gathered was to answer such questions as, "Who are we as a parish?" and "What do we want to become in the future?" The team met with the staff, the pastoral council and the parish as a whole through open forums and town halls. These meetings sought to answer three questions:

1. What do we have in the parish that we want to keep, nourish and celebrate?

2. What are we willing to let go of, adjust or eliminate?

3. What new things do we want to add, try out, give new energy to, bring to reality in the parish?

As a result of this dialoguing, the parish profiles developed by the transition teams were meant to be more comprehensive than the traditional parish reports, which tended to deal only with numbers, finance, personnel, programs and buildings. The profiles developed by the teams were to include the hopes and dreams of the people and to identify the commitment the parish community was willing to make to a new pastor. These parish profiles would eventually be shared with the prospective pastors and assist them in their discernment process.

Other requirements of the transition team came into play during the second phase, or "time-out period," when there would be no assigned pastor in the parish. The diocese would see to it that a priest was assigned for sacramental ministry only. The transition team, along with the staff and council, would assume the temporary role of "pastoring" the parish, by ritual, prayer, formal and informal sharings to help people internalize what was happening. A variety of issues may be addressed during this time, depending on the length of the interim period. In some of the parishes involved in the pilot project, the prospective pastors met with the parish transition team to discuss the parish profile. The priests said later that they found this extremely helpful. The transition team that used the empty suitcase moved it to the presider's chair in the sanctuary during the interim period to symbolize the absence of a pastor. All of the teams we worked with called the parishioners to pray for the guidance of the Spirit in the upcoming appointment and for an openness of heart in accepting the new pastor.

During the third phase, the transition teams were required to become the eyes and ears of the new pastor in the parish. After the formal ritual of installation and welcoming, which the teams helped plan and orchestrate, they were to stay in operation for two to three more months to provide feedback to the pastor on how he was being perceived by parishioners. Some of the teams took him out for coffee or to lunch, or met with him in the rectory once or twice a month to share with him the good things they were hearing, as well as any hints of misunderstandings or negative reactions. The effectiveness of this approach varied among the teams involved in the pilot. Some felt they needed more help in learning the skills of giving feedback, while others questioned how receptive the pastor was to what they had to share with him. From the experience with the pilot, we remain committed to the concept of giving feedback, but we feel that more time needs to be given to training the teams for this task. We also saw a need to work with the new pastors so that this aspect of the process could prove to be beneficial.

All the pieces are now in place to begin the process. The diocesan committee is formed and the members have been assigned as resources and contact persons for individual parishes. The outgoing pastors have agreed to participate in the process and have appointed a transition team to carry the parish through the change. The teams themselves are aware of what will be expected ofu them during each phase of the transition. All that remains is to begin the transition process itself.

Note: At the end of this and subsequent chapters we have included handout materials that we used during the pilot project. We offer them as resources for those wishing to adapt this process to their own situation.

Transition Process Goals

1. For Leaving Pastors:

   That they have a chance to say good-bye in a way that will put effective closure on their pastorates while giving them a sense of support and a vision for a growthful future.

2. For Parishes:

   That they have a yearlong structured process to use in coping with transition when a pastor is leaving. This process will guide them throughout the period of change with thoughtful deliberation. The process will include time for new beginnings with new leadership.

3. For Prospective Pastors:

   That new or transitioning pastor candidates, or those considering a change of parishes, have the opportunity to identify their own dreams and expectations and what type of parish could effectively fulfill them.

4. For the Diocese:

   That those responsible for filling open pastorates may learn another option for placement of pastors that addresses the needs of all concerned: outgoing pastors, parishioners and parish staffs, and prospective pastors.

Expectations of the Diocesan Committee

1. Be the primary communicators to parishes and pastors

2. Attend the preliminary planning meeting and the workshops

3. Provide location and setup for workshops

4. Provide accommodations and local transportation for outside facilitators

5. Duplicate and distribute materials sent by the facilitators for the process

6. Maintain constant contact with the facilitators and provide feedback

7. Let the facilitators know about existing and potential snags

8. Read background materials on transition provided by the facilitators

9. Meet periodically as a committee to keep the process moving forward

Expectations for the Departing Pastor

1. To identify and appoint the parish transition team according to the guidelines

2. To attend the two diocesan workshops in January and June

3. To design the leave-taking ritual with the help of the staff, leaders and transition team

4. To support the transition team in its tasks by giving it the freedom to function

5. To take time to say good-bye to significant individuals and groups

6. To allow time for grieving and letting go and to make room for new possibilities

7. To leave the parish and its operation in reasonably good order

8. To take time off following the leave-taking in order to prepare for the future

Guidelines for the Parish Transition Team

Suggested Size: Seven to twelve people

Suggested Composition:

A. One staff member (not the pastor)

B. One council member (not the chairperson)

C. Two or three persons active in parish ministries or commissions

D. One or two persons with experience in previous parish transitions

E. Two members from the parish community who are not involved in leadership

Transition Team Profile:

A. Members should have some experience in:

1. Working with groups

2. Listening skills

3. Synthesizing information

4. Leading groups

5. Motivating others

6. Talking in front of groups

7. Dealing with conflict

8. Being flexible and noncontrolling

B. Transition Team characteristics:

1. A balance of men, women and diverse age groups

2. A variety of backgrounds that reflects the parish make up

3. People who are accepted and credible in the parish

4. People who are willing and able to attend the three diocesan workshops in January, June and October

5. People who are willing and able to commit themselves to the eleven-month process

6. People who are open to ongoing training during the process

Responsibilities:

  A. To attend the three diocesan workshops during the year

  B. To do the prescribed reading

  C. To discern a chairperson

  D. To describe the transition process to the parish community

  E. To work with the departing pastor and support him during the transition

  F. To help the parish community say good-bye to the departing pastor in ritual and celebration

  G. To call the people to pray for the guidance of the Spirit in every phase of the transition

  H. To gather information about the current state of the parish and about people's hopes and expectations, using resources available from the diocese

  J. To process and synthesize this information and produce a brief report about the parish

  I. To prepare periodic reports of the team's activities to be shared with the parish leadership and people, as well as with the diocesan transition committee

  K. To encourage the staff and council in providing continuity during the interim phase of the transition

  L. To provide information about the new pastor to the parish community prior to the pastor's arrival

  M. To prepare the parish community for welcoming the new pastor in ritual and celebration

  N. To act as a resource to the new pastor during the initial stages of the new pastorate

  O. To give feedback to the new pastor about how people are responding

  P. To ask help of the diocesan transition committee when needed

  Q. To acquaint the new pastor with the current operation of the parish

Chapter Four

Preparing to Say Good-bye

The transition process began with the first set of workshops for the outgoing pastors, the transition teams and prospective pastors. The goals of these workshops were to explore and develop attitudes about transition, to help the people deal with the transition of pastors prayerfully and reflectively, to acquaint them with all that would be involved in making the transition and to learn the skills that would assist them throughout the process.

Outgoing Pastors

Our first session was with the outgoing pastors. It was clear that many of these pastors would prefer to just slip out the back door in the middle of the night and disappear from sight and thought. Our task was to help them understand that for their own and their people's well-being, this was not a wise approach. In prayer, presentations, reflections and sharing of experiences, we kept before them this reality: "If you don't say good-bye to your present situation you won't be able to say hello to what's coming."

The workshop for the pastors was scheduled for 9:30 a.m. to 3:30 p.m. with lunch included. We began with introductions. Although they all knew each other, this gave each person the opportunity to talk about his parish and to tell the group *when* and, if he chose to, *why* he was leaving it.

The opening prayer was planned around the theme of journey. An open suitcase with a growing plant in it, a candle and a Bible helped to set a prayerful tone. We started with brief selections from Genesis and Exodus, followed by a prayer asking the Lord to be the God of the journey. A longer reading from Exodus prepared for a "suitcase reflection." Time was given for each person to reflect on two questions: What blessings of my life do I most want to carry with me as I move on? What blessings am I most in need of as I continue my journey? There was a period of sharing and a final prayer of thanksgiving asking that we "hold all of life in open hands and treasure all as gift and blessing."

After an overview of this project, we reviewed the following list of **expectations** for the departing pastor and discussed each point briefly.

1. To identify and appoint the parish transition team according to the guidelines.
2. To attend the two diocesan workshops in January and June.
3. To design the leave-taking ritual with the help of the staff, parish leaders and transition team.
4. To support the transition team in its tasks by giving it the freedom to function.
5. To take time to say good-bye to significant individuals and groups.
6. To allow time for grieving and letting go and to make room for new possibilities.
7. To leave the parish and its operation in reasonable order.
8. To take time off after the leave-taking so as to prepare for the future.

The pastors were then asked to recall what it was like for them when they first came to the parish they were now preparing to leave. The stories ranged from sad to funny to touching. One man told of how incredibly dirty everything in the rectory was. Another recounted arriving to find the rectory empty of most furniture and even basic necessities, such as linens and dishes. Others told of welcoming parties and good experiences with the departing pastor who spent time walking them through the ins and outs of parish life and introducing them to some of the key folks in the parish. Two questions were then asked: As you leave this parish what do you want to repeat of your experience in coming to the parish for your successor? What do you *not* want to repeat? The pastors' discussion of these questions was insightful and mutually helpful.

A presentation was then given on the stages of transition – endings, interim and new beginnings – using the following chart. (See Chapter Two, page 10.)

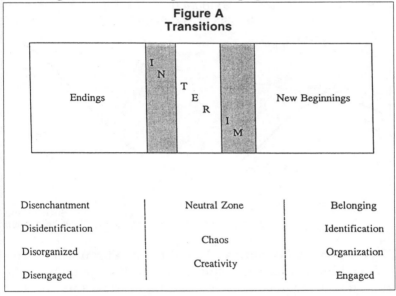

Figure A
Transitions

Endings	INTERIM	New Beginnings
Disenchantment	Neutral Zone	Belonging
Disidentification		Identification
	Chaos	
Disorganized		Organization
	Creativity	
Disengaged		Engaged

The goal was to help the pastors recognize what was going on in their lives as they embarked upon this period of transition, to own their experience of it and to realize how normal it is to be going through these stages.

To feel disenchanted, to experience disidentification, to be disorganized and even disengaged is what happens when a part of one's life and ministry is known to be coming to an end. To deny this ending is to miss what it has to teach. The Neutral Zone, the betwixt and between time, the *not-*

here-but-not-quite-there time follows. This can be a period of chaos as efforts are made to adjust to the changes. It also has the potential for being a period of great creativity and high energy. The final stage is to embrace the new beginnings so as to experience belonging and a new identification, to once again be capable of organizing tasks, making commitments and engaging with the new reality.

A further explanation was given using a graphic from *Life Changes* by Sabina Spencer and John Adams explained in Chapter Two. (See page 10, Figure A.)

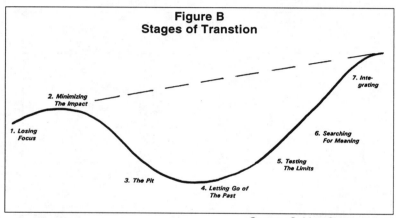

Figure B
Stages of Transtion

Source: Sabina Spencer and John Adams, *Life Changes*, Impact Publishers, 1990

Transition usually causes a loss of focus. This normal experience is particularly difficult to deal with for someone who is used to being in control, a reality for most pastors. Routine situations are suddenly confused, and the unexpected keeps happening. This is not a comfortable time. The natural tendency is to do whatever it takes to minimize the impact and move as quickly and painlessly as possible right to the integration stage. But it doesn't work! Notice the broken lines on the way over. Someplace along the way the inevitable happens. The person slips between the cracks and falls into the pit. It is better to recognize the pit and surrender to it for as long as it takes to make the adjustments. The pit is part of the necessary grieving for the past. Staying too long in the pit, however, is not healthy either. It is important to let go of the past, both the good and the not-so-good relationships, places and events. As this happens, it is possible to test the limits of the new situation and look for new meaning in all that has been happening during the transition period. It is this search for meaning that results in a reintegration of the new with the old.

The pastors easily identified with the pit experience. This led to a fruitful discussion of how such experiences had been handled in the past, not always with the best results. It also gave them insight into how this transition out of the parish might be more productive and growth producing.

Associated with the stages of transition are several tasks that the pastors were asked to contemplate. These tasks include:

acknowledging and accepting the loss,

reviewing and evaluating the past,

discerning what to hold onto and what to let go,

considering and consolidating options for the future.

The pastors were then given large sheets of newsprint and were asked to develop a history line of their pastorate. This meant listing all the significant events that took place in the parish during their pastorates. Then they were asked to share them with the group. We also asked permission to share the time lines with the transition teams later that evening. The pastors found this a most rewarding experience as they had a chance to identify the highlights of their pastorates and to tell their stories to others. Once they got started, it was difficult keeping them within the time limit.

The next presentation was on saying good-bye. We drew heavily from Joyce Rupp's book *Praying Our Good-byes* (Notre Dame: Ave Maria Press, 1988). Starting with the precept that *if we don't say good-bye we cannot say hello,*we explored the richness of the word "good-bye." Originally it was a greeting: "God be with ye!" It was a blessing of love that indicated that God was a significant part of the leaving. The

One who gives and cherishes life would be present on the journey to protect and to console the person. If God went with you, you would never be alone.

Saying good-bye signifies an empty place within, some kind of loss or incompleteness, a space waiting to be filled, a hollow feeling deep inside. Looking at it this way made it clear that good-byes open up spaces for reflection and conversion, and that major good-byes, such as taking leave of a parish, evoke significant questions:

Why must there be suffering?

Where is life taking me?

What are my most cherished values?

What do I believe about life after death?

Good-byes are integral to life. Their stories are inside of us, stories of gain and loss, joy and sorrow, life and death, union and separation. The cycle of good-byes begins at birth when we were pushed to say farewell to the safety and comfort of the womb and cried hello to a vastly different world. All life long we say our good-byes: to family, friends, places, ministries, security, health, ideas, dreams and ultimately to life itself. Sometimes we choose our good-byes and at other times they choose us. Only if we let go are we free to move on. Without this intentionality we fail to practice for the final step of our homeward journey.

Because good-byes reveal a great deal about the significant others in our lives, we asked the pastors to reflect on the following questions:

Who will walk the long road with me?

Who will love me in good times and in bad?

Whose heart will always welcome me?

The final point made in this presentation was that we must learn to acknowledge the pain of transitions and move on if we are to say a genuine hello to the future. The pastors were then asked to reflect quietly on these questions and then share their insights with one other person in the group. By then it was time for lunch.

After lunch the pastors worked with the following reflection sheet:

Saying Good-bye

Consider the times in your life when you have said good-bye. List three or four.

Which ones were good experiences? Why?

Which ones were painful experiences? Why?

What made the difference between good and bad?

Which good-bye in your life was the *most* growthful? Why?

What was it like the last time you left a parish?

What was it like when you came to your present parish?

What good-byes have you already said in the parish? What ones remain? How can you make them experiences for life and growth? Who can help you do this?

At this time of your life, what do you see as the greatest personal value in the good-bye process?

The pastors had twenty minutes to reflect on these questions and to jot down ideas and insights. We did not discuss the results of this reflection. Rather, we asked that they take the sheet home, pray over it and share it with a friend, a co-worker or a spiritual director.

We spent the rest of the day discussing some practical issues, including the following.

1. What to leave behind? We discussed the importance of leaving the parish financial records in order, of terminating a difficult staff member rather than leaving this for the next pastor, of making adjustments in the Mass schedules. This was summed up in the admonition to make sure that there were no painful or messy surprises for the new person.

2. The role of the transition team and its interaction with the pastor. We encouraged the pastors to stay in touch with the team and give them support and freedom in gathering information for the parish report.

3. Planning the ritual for leave-taking, allowing people sufficient time to say good-bye.

4. Planning the interim period in the parish, lining up priests to handle the Masses and sacraments, seeing to it that people know what is expected of them and what tasks belong to which group.

At the end of the session we gave each pastor the booklet *Running through the Thistles,* by Roy M. Oswald (Washington, D.C.: The Alban Institute, 1978). This is a reflection and practical guide on how to terminate a ministerial relationship with a parish. The value of this booklet was recognized by all who used it. We recommend it as a most worthy resource.

The closing prayer consisted of spontaneous petitions asking for God's blessing on all those involved in transition.

Parish Transition Teams

The sessions for the parish transition teams were held on two consecutive evenings from 7:30 to 9:30. By way of introduction we asked each person to give his or her name, parish and a brief statement about accepting the invitation to be on the team. Although we had not anticipated it, a clear and consistent message became obvious in the reasons people gave for joining the team. While it is true that most of the laity do not have the theological language that identifies them as the People of God, it was undeniable as we listened to them speak, that they had, for the most part, internalized that teaching of Vatican II. Over and over again they spoke of the parish being their responsibility. The work they did over the next ten months would prove that they meant what they were saying!

The prayer used that first evening was for guidance. It stressed the need for wisdom, courage and a deep commitment to carry out their mission. Once again the open suitcase with a growing plant in it and a candle served as the focal point in the prayer space. After reading the same Exodus passage used for the pastors (Ex. 13:17-22), the following prayer.

> God of the exodus, we are on a road never traveled before. Deep within, where only you can see, there is much mystery, grayness and restlessness. We seek a sense of direction, to know where you need us to be headed. Be our signpost. Let your wisdom guide us and let us trust always in your promise, "do not fear. I go before you." We ask this in the name of Jesus. Amen.

Using the same diagram we had used with the pastors, we presented an overview of the transition process, (see pages 38-39). Added to the overview was a listing of the responsibilities of the parish transition team:

1. To attend the three diocesan workshops during the year

2. To do the prescribed reading

3. To discern a chairperson *(not a staff member)*

4. To describe the transition process to the parish community

5. To work with the departing pastor and support him during the transition

6. To help the parish community say good-bye to the departing pastor in ritual and celebration

7. To call the people to pray for the guidance of the Spirit in every phase of the transition

8. To gather information about the current state of the parish and about the people's hopes and expectations, using the resources available from the diocese

9. To process and synthesize this information and produce a brief report about the parish

10. To prepare periodic reports of the team's activities to be shared with the parish leadership and people, as well as with the diocesan transition committee

11. To encourage the staff and council in providing continuity during the interim phase of the transition

12. To provide information about the new pastor to the parish community prior to the pastor's arrival

13. To prepare the parish community for welcoming the new pastor in ritual and celebration

14. To act as a resource to the new pastor during the initial stages of the new pastorate

15. To give feedback to the new pastor about how people are responding

16. To ask help of the diocesan contact person when needed

17. To acquaint the new pastor with the current operation of the parish

Next came a presentation on the phases of the transition process and the scope of the team's job during each phase. Recognizing that the phases overlap to some degree, we explained that in the first phase, the "ending" period, their task was to support the leave-taking of the pastor, help the parish say good-bye and guide the parish in praying for the guidance of the Spirit. This was the time they would be gathering information about the parish and producing a report for the diocese and the prospective pastors.

During the "in-between," or interim, phase, the team helps shepherd the parish through the difficult period of letting go and waiting for the new pastor. This can also be a graced moment for the parish to look at "Who are we and what makes us unique?" The team is expected to be the stabilizing element during this time, but also the one raising important questions for parishioners to reflect on. At this time the team provides information on the new pastor once he is appointed.

During the final, or "new beginnings," stage, the team is there to hold things together, to prepare the welcome of the new pastor, to help with the welcoming ceremony and celebration, to act as a resource to the pastor and to be the eyes and ears of the parish, providing the pastor with feedback and insights about how people are responding to the new leadership.

Describing the team's role during the three phases of the transition led to a presentation on their immediate task of helping the pastor and the parish say good-bye to one another. Using the same material on saying good-bye presented to the pastors, each parish group discussed how it might assist both the pastor and the people to accomplish this important function.

A second immediate task for the transition team is to gather information about the parish in preparation for the report. This is critical work. Six steps for the gathering of data guide this critical part of the work.

1. First, prepare the materials for the infomation-gathering sessions. Key questions for reflection about the parish include: What do we need to keep? What do we need to let go of? What do we need to develop, begin, create for the future? What gifts, qualities, talents do we need in a leader to help us move toward our vision? What gifts, qualities, talents do the people of this parish bring to such a vision?

2. Conduct a preliminary session with the staff and council and key leaders. They begin by explaining the steps involved in transition. Then they ask people to reflect individually on the five questions listed above. Next they divide the staff and leaders into small groups for sharing and noting common ideas. Then the team gathers all the staff and leaders together to share the results of the small group discussion and to record the insights for later use in the parish report.

3. Hold a series of town hall meetings for the entire parish. The town halls are be scheduled at different times. People from different backgrounds and various ages are encouraged to attend. The agenda for the town halls would follow the same format as the leader-

ship's session, including the use of small groups. The staff, council and lay leaders act as facilitators of the small groups. The results from these town halls are recorded for use in the final report.

4. Provide an opportunity for those who did not attend the town halls to give their insights by inserting reflection sheets with the five questions into the bulletin or by mailing them to parishioners for their response.

5. Analyze the results from leaders and parishioners in order to discover common threads. The team then calls a second meeting with staff and lay leaders to share the information gathered in the parish and to reflect with them on "What makes us special or different as a parish?" The results of the information gathering may be published in the bulletin or parish newsletter for all to see.

6. Using all this information, prepares a brief fifteen- to twenty-page report, that includes:

   • general information and background about the parish – its size, history and makeup,

   • what is unique or special about the parish,

   • the current structure of the staff, council, ministry groups and organizations,

   • a summary of what to keep, what to let go of, what to start anew.

This report is given to the diocesan contact person or to the personnel board of the diocese. The transition teams are encouraged to request assistance from the diocesan transition committee contact person anytime during the process if they need help or assistance.

A *word of caution* must be noted here. No matter how many times it is said, there will be people who see this process as a way to name the new pastor. This is *not* the intent. At no time are potential pastors interviewed by the transition team or parish leaders as a means of picking a replacement. It was our experience that this fact needed to be said over and over again to prevent any false expectations from arising.

After a break, each parish transition team prepared a history line of the present pastorate identifying the key moments during this period, both ups and downs. We then asked permission from each team to share this history line with the pastors.

The final task of the evening was to fashion a prayer to be used during the time of transition in the parish. The parishioners would be praying this prayer on a regular basis during the coming months.

What follows are three prayers developed by the transition teams in each of the three dioceses participating in the pilot project.

Prayer 1: Loving, tender God, we seek your wisdom! We need your help! Let us be grateful for the pastor who has guided and called us to where we are now as a parish. Let him know that he is loved. Show us how to let go of him and be open to the future. Help us to be welcoming to the new pastor who will soon be with us. Let us open our hearts and arms to embrace him, accept his leadership and support his efforts. Be with the transition team of our parish. Give them wisdom, courage and the energy they will need to move us through this important time of transition. May all of this bring us closer to you and closer to each other. We ask this, O God, in the name of your son, Jesus, and the spirit of love. Amen.

Prayer 2: Loving and compassionate God, help us to stay open to your guidance and to trust that you want what is best for our parish. May the new pastor continue to empower the members of our parish and may we, the parishioners, be generous and supportive as we begin this new journey. Help us to let go of the pastor we now cherish and make room for the new pastor who is to come. Let us trust, O God, that all things do work together for the good of us, your people. Amen.

Prayer 3: Almighty and loving God, we ask your guidance during this time of transition. Bless our pastor as he leaves our parish. May he know our gratitude for his years of service. May his new ministry be graced and may bring him joy. Bless us, the members of this parish. May we forgive ourselves and one another for past mistakes and failures and let go of our hurts and disappointments. Bless our transition team as they help us during this important time. May they listen to us and to the spirit. Bless the new pastor who will come to us. May he find acceptance and support and may he challenge us to continue to grow. Send your spirit upon us to touch our hearts and lead us to you. Amen.

Before the teams left that first evening session, they were given a reflection sheet and asked to come the next evening ready to share their thoughts with one another. The sheet asked the following questions:

What do we need to keep?

What do we need to let go of for the future?

What do we need to develop, begin, create for the future?

What gifts, qualities, talents do we need in a leader that would help us move toward our vision?

What gifts, qualities and talents do the people of this parish bring to such a process?

This homework included the same questions they would be asking their leaders and people later in the process. This was their chance to reflect on these questions before asking others to do so.

When the teams returned the next day for the second evening session, they began with a simple rebonding exercise and then moved into prayer. Considering the reflection they had done following the previous evening's session, people were asked to formulate prayers of petition to which all would respond: LET YOUR WISDOM BE WITH US, O LORD! The petitions centered on aspects of the parish that the team members felt worth keeping, letting go of and starting anew.

A presentation followed on the theme of *letting go of the tone: how to let someone you like (or don't like) leave.* Much of what we presented to the group came from Joyce Rupp's insights in *Praying Our Good-byes.* The goal was to increase awareness among team members around the task of saying good-bye. Six important insights were identified:

1. It is next to impossible to let go of anyone or anything unless we first let go of whatever binds us to the past, whether it be a heavy burden that creates a sad atmosphere or a memory that gnaws at our peace of mind. These things stir up negative feelings, sap our energy and cloud our vision.

2. Sometimes we choose to cling to deadness and lack of life rather than face the unknown. This is called escapism, and it is never a healthy behavior. The challenge is to redirect our energy, to look to what is life giving and not to concentrate on what was hurtful in the past.

3. This does not imply denying past hurts. But it does mean that we must accept what has been and move on!

4. Simply put, we must give up old securities that bind us, painful memories that harm us, dashed dreams that discourage us, and heartbreaking wounds that keep us from dreaming.

5. We may also have to let go of the fear that no matter how good the future will be, it can't measure up to the past. Such self-fulfilling prophecies are just that!

6. Letting go does not mean blocking out all memories. As we let go, we need to cherish the good memories and all the people who caused them to happen.

Both the outgoing pastors and the transition teams had developed parish timelines. At the second evening session, team members were given their pastor's timeline to compare with their own. Some teams discovered great similarities between the two time lines. Others were amazed at what had been important to the pastor or at his interpretations of certain events, which were quite different from theirs. For some it was an opportunity to recognize why difficulties had arisen over priorities and projects. Perceptions were so different that it was obvious why misunderstandings had occurred. Following this experience the team members were given quiet time to reflect prayerfully on what it would be like to start again with new leadership and to have a better sense of expectations, dreams and desires on the part of both the new pastor and the parish at large. This clarity of expectations would be one result of this transition process as it p□7gressed through the ending, the in-between and the beginning stages.

A discussion followed on how the transition teams might help the outgoing pastor put closure to his pastorate. We shared the same suggestions presented to the pastors about how to say good-bye, about putting things in order before he leaves and ritualizing the leave-taking ceremonies. The entire group did brainstorming on ways the teams could be useful and supportive to the pastor in this process.

After a break we turned to the task of gathering information for the parish reports. One way to gather information was to hold a town hall or open forum for all interested parishioners. Care must be taken in leading these gatherings to make them a positive experience for all and not an outlet for criticism or a communal gripe session.

A brief presentation followed on what *not* to do with town halls or open forums. For instance, the way questions are asked is critical to the validity of the information received. To ask people what they *think* about any given issue or topic is dangerous because people tend to think in negatives. If the leader says, "What do you *think* about . . .?" most people will decode the question in their heads and hear, "What don't you like about . . .?" That is what they will tell you and perhaps all they will tell you. The first question asked of people should put a positive spin on the topic: "What do you like? What do you want us to keep?" The second question begins to get at the negatives when you ask, "If you could change something, what would it be and *how* would you do it?" Then comes the creative question, "If you could add something, what would it be and *how* would you do it?"

If the group is larger than twenty or thirty, it is important to break it into smaller discussion groups. People tend to resist this movement, saying that they want to hear what everyone has to say. The best way *not* to hear from everyone, however, is to stay in a large group in which many are afraid or unwilling to speak. Far better to use small groups and have reporters prepared to give brief reports to the large gathering.

The transition teams were reminded of the importance of making it clear that the parishioners would not be choosing their pastor. Rather, the people would help develop a profile of the parish, which in turn would attract the leader they needed and prayed for.

At the conclusion of the session, the teams were sent off to their tasks with the reminder that they had a backup system called the diocesan transitional committee and that they should not hesitate to call on their designated contact person from that committee as often as they felt the need.

Prospective Pastors Workshops

The workshop for the prospective pastors was held in the morning following the second evening session for transition teams. It began at 9:00 a.m. and lasted until noon. Each diocese determined how it would extend the invitation and to whom it would be extended. Some of the people attending were associate pastors seeking their first pastorate. Others were pastors whose tenure was coming to an end or who were seeking a change. In some cases, the diocese asked people to attend the workshop because they would be good candidates for the open parishes. They may or may not choose to change positions at this time but they were encouraged to at least think about it. In one diocese, a number of men and women who had been certified for the position of pastoral administrator were present for this session. It was wonderful to have the mix of ordained and nonordained. They discovered so much about each other and their shared hopes and fears. However, their presence at this meeting did set up a false hope in the hearts of many of the nonordained participants. There was no way that many, or perhaps any of them, would be assigned to be the administrator of a parish. Their presence generated a great deal of energy and creativity, but it also left some with strong feelings of disappointment and anger. We learned from this experience that while it is a good thing to include the nonordained pastoral administrators, it must be done with great honesty and openness. The diocese must be clear about what possibilities exist for the placement of nonordained pastoral administrators so that no false expectations are raised.

We began the workshops with introductions, asking each participant to give his or her name and reasons for attending this session. The prayer that followed was the same one used with the outgoing pastors and the transition teams. The empty suitcase with its plant and the candle provided the ambiance for the prayer space.

Next came a review of the *Expectations for Prospective Pastors,* a handout that had been mailed to them along with the invitation to attend the workshop. It outlined the following expectations:

1. To be willing to say they are considering the possibility of a new pastorate

2. To enter into the transition process with a discerning heart

3. To attend the three diocesan workshops in January, June and October

4. To be open to new methods of pastoral placement

5. To articulate their vision for pastoring a parish

6. To be in dialogue with and open to other people's vision of pastoring

7. To discern which parishes might fit the person's vision and talents

8. To plan the welcoming ritual in the new parish, in consultation with the staff, leaders and transition team

9. To be open to the input and insights of the transition team

10. To take time to be reflective about the parish and about one's own leadership style during the first few months of pastoring

11. To recognize the importance of the "tone" that a new pastor establishes in the parish

12. To be open to the adjustment of one's own hopes and dreams and to call the parish community to this same flexibility

There followed the same overview of the transition process presented to the outgoing pastors and the transition teams, along with an explanation of what was new about this pilot project and the special emphasis on the role of the transition teams that new pastors would be inheriting and how these teams could be helpful to them.

We then asked: "What do you need to say good-bye to in order to say hello to a new ministry?" There was much discussion around who, what, when, where and how these good-byes could happen, along with a strong recommendation to plan break time, a vacation or a mini-sabbatical before taking on any new assignment.

After a break, the participants were given the following work sheet to guide them through a reflection on their vision of pastoring a parish:

My Ideal Parish Would Look Like This

1. What might be its size, location and makeup? Would it have a school?

2. What would the staff look like in terms of its size, positions, roles, type of interaction?

3. How would the liturgies be conducted, format, environment, music, number per weekend?

4. What would be the parish's predominant emphasis or focus?

5. What would your leadership focus be like?

After half an hour of private reflection, we asked them to recall their last move and consider three questions: What don't you want to repeat this time around? What do you want to hold on to? What do you want to create anew? They shared results of their reflection with one other person. Then, recognizing that the "perfect" parish does not exist, we distributed a work sheet that asked them to list what was negotiable and what was not negotiable for them as they looked ahead at possible placements and in studying the parish reports prepared by the transition teams. This generated a great deal of discussion among the prospective pastors and provided a guide for their future considerations and decision making.

During this discussion we stressed the importance of not imposing one's own model of parish on parishioners but rather entering into a dance of leaders and people as they assume the new position. They needed to respect and accept what the people wanted to hold on to, let go of and start anew. The parish did not "belong" to the new pastor, in other words.

The final hour of the morning dealt with many practical tasks. We spoke of letting go of their present situation and what this implied. For example, does a pastor go "back" to a former parish to preside at weddings, funerals or baptisms? No, except in extraordinary circumstances. To nurture friendships among those you have left is one thing but to continue to function as "their priest" was recognized as unacceptable.

The prospective pastors were then asked to fill out a reflection sheet on seeking to discern God's will. The questions on discernment included:

1. What gifts would I bring to the ministry of pastoring?

2. What needs do I have?

3. What excites or challenges me about pastoring?

4. What fears do I have?

5. What clues do I have that the spirit is calling me to be a pastor (or change my place of pastoring)?

6. What am I willing to let go of in order to enter into this ministry (or change my place of pastoring)?

Participants were encouraged to use this as a personal and prayerful reflection exercise during the weeks and months ahead. Once again we stressed the importance of taking time off between assignments, acknowledging that this was perhaps a new concept for them that some might not view kindly. We felt, however, that it was a necessary step toward a fruitful and graceful transition.

Reminding them of the work they had done earlier on their ideal parish, we suggested that they look at possible options in terms of first and second choices so as not to limit either themselves or the Spirit. We also discussed the possibility of disappointment if they were not given the parish of their choice and how to handle their feelings of not being in control of such a vital area of their lives.

The prospective pastors were asked to consider having a mentor, someone who had a positive experience of pastoring and could act as a sounding board for their reflection and insight. Most thought this was a wise approach. Some of the dioceses we worked with already had such a mentoring program in place.

Finally we talked about the parish reports they would be receiving within a few months for their consideration. We helped them focus on what they should be looking for and what to be aware of as they reflected on the reports. The session closed with prayers of petition for themselves and for those parishes that would soon be experiencing transitions, both the ones they might be leaving and new ones they might be joining.

At the conclusion of the three workshops, the real work of transition began. The outgoing pastors returned to their parishes equipped with ways of saying good-bye. The transition teams geared up for preparing parish reports. The prospective pastors began the discerning process of whether this was the time to move, and if so, where they would like to go.

Outgoing Pastors' Workshop Agenda Time:
(9:30 a.m. to 3:30 p.m.)

Introductions

Prayer

Overview of transition process
   What the transition into the parish was like
   What to repeat
   What not to repeat

History line of the pastorate individually on newsprint
   Comparing the experiences

Break

Saying good-byes
   Implications and options

Prayerful reflection on the material
   Personal time and group time

Lunch

How to say good-bye to the parish
   How and to Whom
   When
   Areas of reconciliation

Practical issues
   What to leave and not to leave behind (no surprises)
   The role of the transition team and its interaction
   with you
   Planning the ritual of leave-taking
   Planning the interim period in the parish

Closure, preparing a prayer for the parish during transition

A Prayer for the Journey

"Where have you come from and where are you going?"
(Gen. 16:8)

LEADER: YAHWEH GUARDS ME FROM HARM

ALL: AND GUARDS MY LIFE.
GOD GUARDS MY LEAVING AND MY COMING BACK
NOW AND FOREVER (Gen. 16:8)

LEADER: I, YOUR GOD, SHALL BE WITH YOU

ALL: I HAVE VISITED YOU
I WILL FREE YOU FROM SLAVERY
I WILL ADOPT YOU AS MY OWN
I WILL BE YOUR GOD (Ex. 3)

LEADER: LET US PRAY:

GUARDIAN AND GUIDE, WE SENSE YOUR PRESENCE WITH US, GOD OF THE JOURNEY. YOU WALK WITH US INTO A NEW LAND. YOU ARE GUARDING US IN OUR VULNERABLE MOMENTS.

YOU ARE PROMISING US PEACE AS WE FACE THE STRUGGLES AHEAD, THE PLANTING OF FEET AND HEARTS IN NEW PLACES.

RENEW IN US A DEEP TRUST IN YOU. CALM OUR ANXIOUSNESS. AS WE REFLECT ON OUR LIVES, HELP US TO REALIZE THAT YOU HAVE BEEN PRESENT IN ALL OF OUR LEAVINGS AND COMINGS. LET US PLACE OUR LIVES INTO THE WELCOMING ARMS OF YOUR LOVE.

ENCIRCLE OUR HEARTS WITH YOUR PEACE. MAY YOUR POWERFUL PRESENCE RUN LIKE A STRONG THREAD THROUGH THE FIBERS OF OUR BEINGS.

ALL: AMEN
(READING: Ex. 13:17-22)

Suitcase Reflection: Quiet Reflection

LEADER: IT IS ALMOST SUITCASE PACKING TIME. AS WE PREPARE TO PACK OUR BELONGINGS, LET US CONSIDER:
WHAT BLESSINGS OF MY LIFE DO I MOST WANT TO CARRY WITH ME AS I MOVE ON? WHAT BLESSINGS AM I MOST IN NEED OF AS I CONTINUE MY JOURNEY?

LEADER: LET US PRAY:

ALL: WE GIVE YOU PRAISE, GOD OF OUR JOURNEY, FOR THE POWER OF LOVE, THE DISCOVERY OF FRIENDS, THE MIRACLE OF LIFE, THE FAITH THAT IS STRONGER THAN DISCOURAGEMENT AND ANXIETY.

WE GIVE YOU THANKS, GOD OF OUR JOURNEY, FOR THOSE WHO STAND NEAR, FOR THE DESIRE TO CONTINUE ON, FOR BELIEVING THAT YOU, GOD, CARE FOR US IN OUR VULNERABILITY.

WE ASK FORGIVENESS, GOD OF OUR JOURNEY, FOR HOLDING TOO TIGHTLY, FOR OUR INSISTENCE THAT WE BE SECURE, FOR TAKING ALL THE GOODNESS BUT BEING RELUCTANT TO SHARE IT.

WE BEG YOUR HELP, GOD OF OUR JOURNEY, TO BELIEVE BEYOND THIS MOMENT, TO HOLD ALL OF LIFE IN OPEN HANDS, TO TREASURE ALL AS GIFT AND BLESSING. AMEN.

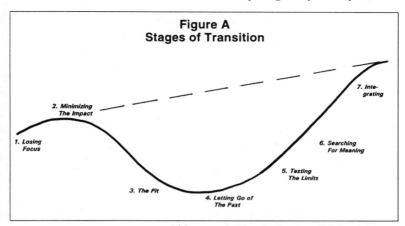

Figure A
Stages of Transition

Source: Sabina Spencer and John Adams,
Life Changes, (Impact Publishers, 1990)

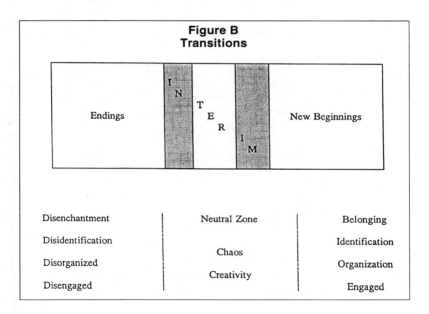

Figure B
Transitions

Endings	Neutral Zone	New Beginnings
Disenchantment		Belonging
Disidentification	Chaos	Identification
Disorganized		Organization
Disengaged	Creativity	Engaged

Transitioning Pastors:
A Note Taker's Outline for Saying Good-bye
If we don't say good-bye, we cannot say hello!

God-be-with-ye
    A blessing of love
    God was a significant part of the going
    The one who gave and cherished life
        would be there to protect and console
    If God went with you, you'd never be alone . . .

What is a good-bye?
    An empty place in us
    Some kind of loss, incompleteness
    A space waiting to be filled
    A hollow feeling, some place deep inside

Good-byes open up spaces for reflection and conversion!

Major good-byes bring us to the big questions:
    Why suffering?
    Where is life taking me?
    What are my most cherished values?
    What do I believe about life after death?

Good-byes are a part of life. The stories are inside of us.
    Gain and loss
    Joy and sorrow
    Life and death
    Union and separation

The cycle begins at birth!
    We pushed farewell to safety and comfort
    and cried hello to a vastly different world.

We started to practice early on!

All life long we say good-byes to

family	friends	places	ministries	life
security	health	ideas	dreams	

Sometimes we choose our good-byes; sometimes they choose us!

Only when we let go are we free to move on . . .

Without this intentionality we fail to practice for the final step of our homeward journey!

Good-byes reveal a lot about the significant others in our lives.
> Who will walk the long road with me?
> Who will love me in good times and bad?
> Whose heart will always welcome me?

We must learn how to acknowledge the pain
> and move on if we are
> to say another hello!

Saying Good-bye in Order to Say Hello
A Prayerful Reflection for Outgoing Pastors

1. To whom do I need to say good-bye?

When?

How?

2. Of what must I let go?

When?

How?

3. What break time will I plan for myself?

When?

Where?

With whom?

Practical Issues for Outgoing Pastors

1. What to leave and not leave behind

2. You and the transition team

3. The ritual of leave-taking (when and how)

4. Planning the interim period (who's in charge for how long?)

Transition Team Workshop Agenda

SESSION ONE (7:30 p.m. to 9:50 p.m.)

Introductions and why you accepted this task

Prayer

Overview of the transition process
  Where the transition team fits in

Three phases
  Scope of the job in each phase (phases overlap)
  Endings: Support leave-taking/help parish say
  good-bye/pray
  In-between: Gather information/produce a report/
  provide support
          Who are we, what makes us unique?
          Information on new pastor
  Beginnings: Prepare welcome/help new pastor with
  welcoming/be resource and ears for new pastor/
  give feedback

Present focus
  Help the pastor and parish say good-bye well
  Gather information about the parish for new
  appointment

Break

History line of the pastorate: Ups and downs
  Key questions
          What to keep, hold on to, maintain
          What to let go, let die, say good-bye to
          What to begin or develop, bring to life
          introduce
  Qualities of a leader to help us do this

How to let someone you like (or don't like) leave
Letting go of the tone

Good-byes: What's involved

Reflection for the interim until second session

SESSION TWO (7:30 p.m. to 9:30 p.m.)

Rebonding

Prayer on one's unique gifts

Sharing pastor's history line from earlier workshop

Helping pastor put closure to the pastorate

Break

Information gathering

Process
       Leaders' meeting as practice run
       Open forum: What to keep, let go, start anew
       Simple survey
       Analysis of information
       Brief report on the present situation of the parish

Hints for survival
       What *not* to do with open forums

Wrap-up

Reflection Sheet for Transition Team Members

1. Why did I agree to be on my parish's transition team?

2. What gifts do I bring to the task?

3. What fears or doubts do I have?

4. What help do I need personally?

5. What help do we need as a team?

Three Overlapping Phases to the Work of the Transition Team

Phase 1: Endings

1. Helping the pastor say good-bye

2. Gathering information from the leaders and the people

Phase 2: Interim

1. Preparing a simple report: Who are we? What makes us unique?

2. Helping parish let go and prepare for new leadership

Phase 3: Beginnings

1. Helping new pastor feel welcome

2. Listening to reactions and providing feedback

The Tasks for Any Period of Transition

1. Acknowledging and accepting loss

2. Reviewing and evaluating the past

3. Discerning what to hold onto and what to let go

4. Considering and consolidating options for the future

(The Transition Team helps the parish accomplish these tasks.)

Transition Team Training
A Personal Reflection Sheet for Team Members

As I consider my experience of this parish:

What do we need to keep?

What do we need to let go of?

What do we need to begin to develop for the future?

What gifts, qualities, talents do we need in a leader to help us move toward our vision?

What gifts, qualities, talents do the people of this parish bring to such a process?

Information Gathering Steps for Parish Transition Team

1. Prepare reflection materials.
   A. What do we need to keep?
   B. What do we need to let go of?
   C. What do we need to develop, begin, create?
   D. What talents or gifts do we need in a new leader?
   E. What talents or gifts do the people need?

2. Do a preliminary session with the staff and council and key leaders.
   A. Begin by explaining a little about transition.
   B. Have people do individual reflection on these questions.
   C. Break into small groups for sharing and noting common ideas.
   D. Regroup to share the results and to explain how to record the insights.

3. Offer a series of town hall meetings for parishioners.
   A. Different times, different groups, different ages.
   B. Use the format described in item 2 (above), including small groups.
   C. Have the staff and lay leaders act as facilitators.
   D. Collect and record the results from the town halls.

4. Provide an opportunity for people who did not attend the town halls to give their insights, perhaps the same reflection sheets included with the bulletin or mailed to parrishioners.

5. Analyze the results from leaders and people to discover the common threads. Have a second meeting with the staff and lay leaders to share the results, then publish the results in the bulletin or newsletter. Ask the leadership to indicate

what is unique about the parish: What makes us special or different?

6. Prepare a brief report on the parish and the reflection sessions. The report should include the following:

A. General information and background (size, history, etc.)

B. What is unique or special about the parish

C. Current structure of staff, council, ministry, groups

D. Current mission statement and goals (if they exist)

E. Summary of what to keep, let go of, start anew

Prospective Pastors' Workshop Agenda
(9:00 a.m. to 12:00 p.m.)

Introductions: Why are you here?

Prayer

Overview on transition
New process/inheriting the transition team

What do you need to say good-bye to in order to say hello?
Who, what, when, where, how
Planning a break time

Break

Your vision of pastoring a parish
Ingredients or aspects

In leaving your present situation or reflecting on your last move
What don't you want to repeat?
What do you want to hang on to?
What do you want to create anew?

In taking on the new pastorate
What is not negotiable? What is negotiable?
Avoid imposing your own model on the parish.
Enter into the dance.

Practical tasks
Letting go of the present situation
How to do discernment about choosing a parish
Having an interval between assignments and ministries
Your ideal parish: first and second choices
Dealing with disappointment and lack of control
Mentoring: finding a person(s) for reflection and insight
Reflecting on the parish reports: what to look for?

Wrap-up (handouts for reflection)

Expectations for the Prospective Pastors

Prospective pastors who are interested in these or other parishes are asked to consider a set of expectations.

1. To be willing to say they are considering the possibility of a new pastorate

2. To enter into the transition process with a discerning heart

3. To attend the three diocesan workshops in January, June and October

4. To be open to new methods of placement

5. To articulate their vision of pastoring a parish

6. To be in dialogue with and open to other people's vision of pastoring

7. To discern the parishes that best fit the person's vision and talents

8. To plan the welcoming ritual in the new parish, in consultation with the staff, leaders and transition team

9. To be open to the input and insights of the transition team

10. To take time to be reflective about the parish and one's own leadership style during the first few months of pastoring

11. To recognize the importance of the "tone" that a new pastor establishes in the parish

12. To be open to the adjustment of one's own hopes and dreams and to call the parish community to this same flexibility

13. To seek out the support and to accept the affirmation of others during the transition process

14. To plan, along with the staff and council, a closing ritual and celebration for the transition team

A Reflection Sheet for Prospective Pastors: My Ideal Parish

1. Description: Its size, location, makeup; with or without a school?

2. Staff: Its size, positions, role, type of interaction

3. Liturgy: Its format, environment, music, how many, at what times

4. The predominant emphasis or focus of parish

5. My leadership emphasis or focus

Work Sheet for Prospective Pastors: Parish Considerations

What is negotiable? | What is not negotiable?

**Personal Reflection Sheet for Prospective Pastors:
Preparing to Move On**

1. What experiences of the past do I not want to repeat?

2. Which of my past experiences do I treasure and want to build on?

3. In my new situation, what would I like to try? How creative do I want to be?

4. What advice would I give to a new pastor (especially if that pastor was like me)?

Take-Home Reflection Sheet for Prospective Pastors

Seeking to discern God's will, prayerfully reflect on the following questions:

1. What gifts do I bring to the ministry of pastoring?

2. What needs do I have?

3. What excites or challenges me about pastoring?

4. What fears do I have?

5. What clues do I have that the Spirit is calling me to be a pastor?

6. What am I willing to let go of in order to enter into this ministry?

Chapter Five

The Chaos and Creativity of the Interim

"Who are you?" asked the caterpillar . . ."
"I – I hardly know, Sir, just at present," Alice replied
rather shyly, "at least I know who I *was* when
I got up this morning, but I think I must
have changed several times since then."
Alice's Adventures in Wonderland
Lewis Carroll

The second round of workshops took place in June. Most of the outgoing pastors had already moved on, or would soon. The transition teams were in the midst of their role of shepherding the parish through the period without a resident pastor. The new pastors already knew or were coming closer to knowing where they would be assigned. This put them all in the in-between, or interim, phase. This is not unlike what Alice called her *"I hardly know, Sir"* place. These workshops were designed to assist all three groups, as well as the parishes, through this period of anxiousness, of not knowing but hoping for the best.

Outgoing Pastors

The outgoing pastors gathered for a morning session. After a chance to rebond and get to know one another again, we moved into prayer for the wisdom and the ability to dream. We asked God to guide and encourage the pastors through the change, that they might be open to hear the Word and be comforted with the wisdom of the Spirit. And so we prayed:

> GOD OF LOVE AND COMPASSION, OPEN OUR
> MINDS AND HEARTS TO YOUR WILL FOR US. LET
> US DREAM DREAMS AND MAKE CHOICES THAT
> WILL BE LIFE GIVING FOR US AND FOR YOUR
> PEOPLE. AMEN.

Spontaneous prayers of petition followed. The conclusion to each petition was "DO NOT LET YOUR HEARTS BE TROUBLED. TRUST! EVEN NOW I AM PREPARING A PLACE FOR YOU."

After reviewing some of the highlights of the January workshop, we asked each pastor to draw up a new history line showing the events of the last five months. We suggested that it probably would not be a straight line. Rather, it was to indicate graphically the ups and downs involved in the transition period thus far. When they completed their work, we had them share their stories with each other, including what worked and what didn't work in their efforts to let go and say good-bye to the parish. We also asked them why some things worked and others did not. This was an affirming experience as they realized how much their stories were alike.

After a break we gave the pastors the following work sheet:

Memo to the New Pastor

Here are a few things I think you need to be aware of as you come to this parish:

About liturgy:

About the folks:

About the staff:

About some possible pitfalls that await you:

And here are some things I can't tell you but wish there was a way for you to find them out:

This is my prayer for you:

After filling out the sheet and sharing it with one other person, we asked them how much of this information they wanted to share with the new pastor and to consider possible ways of doing it.

We then looked at some practical issues and discussed what they had left and not left behind, how they got along with their transition teams, when and how the ritual of leave-taking happened and what provision was being made for the interim period. If the pastor had not as yet left the parish, then all of these issues were still in the present tense and had yet to be accomplished.

The final half-hour was spent reflecting on and sharing with each other what they thought would be the next steps for them and where they might look for new life. We closed with a spontaneous litany of gratitude for all that had happened during their recent pastorate and for all that was yet to come.

Parish Transition Teams

As was the case in January, the transition teams met on two consecutive evenings. The team members came filled with all the activities they had been involved in, with some questions, a few battle scars and much excitement about the future. After a brief period of rebonding we moved into the prayer about dreams, risks and trust. One of the readings struck them as most appropriate to their situation.

NOTHING IS IMPOSSIBLE IF WE PUT ASIDE OUR CAREFUL WAYS, IF WE BUILD DREAMS WITH

FAITH IN OURSELVES, FAITH IN EACH OTHER,
FAITH IN OUR GOD.

As we did with the outgoing pastors, we started with a review of the highlights of the January workshops and then asked each team to draw a history outline of the last six months. The ups and downs were obvious as each team constructed the time line. They then shared with the other teams their own unique experiences of saying good-bye to the pastor, gathering information and writing a parish report. As they told their stories, we asked them to include what worked and what didn't work over the last six months and to share insights about why they did or didn't work.

One concern that was consistent had to do with the parish staffs. It became obvious that we had not adequately included them in the transition process. This caused some discomfort and, in some cases, bad feelings between the staff and the transition team. The misconception that parishes would get to name their pastor continued to surface. Given the history of some of the parishes, there was strong resistance to the belief that what they were doing would make any difference in the naming of their next pastor. The perception was that too often in the past the input from leaders and people was not taken seriously by those responsible for appointing the new pastor. (We will revisit these issues in Chap. 8 in dealing with adaptations and changes to the original process.) As the team members talked and shared across parish lines, many good ideas were offered for dealing with the problems they were facing. It was exciting to see the teams exchanging ideas about creative ways to ritualize the transition time in the parish and handle recurring problems and difficulties.

After the break, each team worked with its diocesan committee contact person to review the parish report they had submitted to the diocese earlier and fill in any gaps or issues not included in the report. Before leaving that first evening, the members were given the following "homework" to prepare them for the next evening's session:

A Prayerful Homework Assignment

List three *hopes* you have for the parish with the new pastor.
1.
2.
3.

List three *concerns* you have as the parish adjusts to the new pastorate.
1.
2.
3.

The second evening with the transition teams began with a prayer ritual that flowed from the homework they had done. Each hope or concern that a person enunciated was followed with: *LET YOUR WISDOM BE WITH US, O LORD.* This prayer mosaic was a touching experience for all the teams to hear as hopes and concerns were shared in the group.

The teams then spent time planning prayer rituals that could be used at the weekend Masses to highlight this period of waiting for the replacement and not knowing what the future might hold. One team decided to place the empty suitcase on the presider's chair in the sanctuary with a stole laid over it as a reminder that they were in an interim between pastors. All agreed that prayers of petition for the person to be named and for the parishioners should be included in the weekend liturgies. Some parishes solicited insights from parishioners about important aspects of the parish that had continued even without a named pastor.

One of the major responsibilities of the transition teams was to be the eyes and ears of the new pastor once he arrived in the parish. Because of this, we made a presentation on feedback skills to prepare them for this task. It was divided into two sections: the art of giving feedback and skills needed for providing feedback.

The Art of Giving Feedback

Feedback can be both *positive* and *negative*. It is usually more helpful to give the positive feedback first.

The *motive* for giving feedback will determine how useful the feedback will be.

The *amount* of feedback given in a single session should be limited to how much the recipient can hear.

Timing and location are critical if feedback is to be accepted gracefully.

Feedback should name the *behavior observed*. The person receiving the feedback should always have the opportunity to respond.

Ongoing *support* should follow in whatever ways seem most helpful to the person receiving the feedback.

Skills Needed for Providing Feedback

Feedback is a communication to a person (or group) which gives that person information about how he or she affects others. Feedback helps an individual consider and alter behaviors and thus achieve goals.

There are eight criteria for useful feedback. As you reflect on them, consider how you give feedback as well as what your experience has been of receiving feedback.

1. Useful feedback is *descriptive* rather than evaluative. It describes the sender's reaction, thus leaving the receiver free to use it or not. By avoiding evaluative language, it reduces the need for the receiver to respond defensively.

2. It is *specific* rather than general. It describes the behavior, not a trait.

3. Its motivation is the *growth* of the receiver, not the satisfaction of the giver. Feedback can be destructive when it serves only the giver's needs.

4. It is directed toward behaviors the receiver *can change.* Frustration is only increased when one is reminded of a shortcoming over which one has no control.

5. It is *solicited* rather than imposed. Feedback is most useful when the receiver asks for assistance.

6. It is well-timed. In general, feedback is most useful when given as soon as possible after the observed behavior.

7. It is checked with the sender. The receiver should be encouraged to rephrase the feedback to ensure clear communication.

8. In a group setting, it is *checked with the group* to discover if it is only one person's perception or if it is shared by others.

The transition teams were then asked to develop a history line of their activities and responsibilities for the next six months. Key moments to be included were the prayer rituals used during the interim period, welcoming the new pastor and team interactions with the new pastor.

The session closed with a prayer for perseverance and a commitment to one another and to the parish to continue this special ministry of shepherding the parish through the transition.

Prospective Pastors: Morning Session

This session was divided into two parts. The morning section was for all newly assigned and prospective pastors. The afternoon session was only for those new pastors who had been assigned to the parishes included in the pilot project.

In the morning session, after rebonding and praying together, the stages of transition were reviewed and all present were asked to share where they were in the process. We then gave a report on the status of the parishes included in the process. Some had already been assigned a new pastor, while others were still waiting to hear who the replacement would be.

Each participant then developed a personal history line of the past six months, including what had been done and what had been left unfinished. Using this time line as a framework, they shared their stories with the entire group, giving reactions and reflections, identifying disappointments and naming where there had been growth and new learnings. Every participant agreed that the process had been one of gaining new insights about themselves and clarifying many of their own expectations, hopes and fears.

The final session of the morning was a presentation on leadership and collaboration as a model for pastoring. We emphasized how essential is the leadership of the pastor, but not as the sole leader or as one "above" or "apart from" other staff members or parish leaders. The pastor's role is to be the bearer of the dream but not his dream alone.

The vision and direction of the parish is worked out in concert with staff and leaders as a reflection of the parish community. It is up to the pastor to provide the framework and support structure to keep this dream and vision alive.

The pastor is also an instigator of change, the person who shakes the foundations and challenges people to step out of the familiar and risk the unfamiliar. This, too, is shared with staff and lay leaders. The constant refrain becomes, "What can we be? To what new future is the Spirit calling us? What needs are not being addressed?"

This leadership task of being bearer of the dream and instigator of change is more essential than administrating programs or handling the daily routine of parish life. Being able to give these duties to others is the measure of a successful pastorate.

Another avenue to success is to create an atmosphere of partnership among staff, council and parish leaders. "We are in this together. Whatever our success or failures, these belong to all of us, not just to the pastor." Too often people speak the words "collaboration" and "partnership" but it is not put into action. To forge a true partnership, the pastor must have a good self-image and a sane estimate of his own capabilities, talents and weaknesses. Only then can the pastor take the risk of letting go and allowing others to take ownership of the parish, its life and its operation. This does not mean the pastor gives up the role of leading but rather that he creates the climate of mutuality and interdependence. Active presence and creative facilitation are the keys to successful pastoring.

Being actively present to the staff, council and parish as a whole means that "I am here as a coworker to learn from you and to be one with you as together we provide for the needs of the people and give direction to the parish. I have duties and obligations to perform, as you do as well. No one person, however, is more important or more essential than another. We all have a part to play and a piece of the wisdom to share."

Being a creative facilitator implies a style of leading that utilizes the talents and gifts of the group for the benefit of the entire parish. The facilitating leader keeps the members on track, challenges them to new insights, holds them accountable for what they agreed to do and maintains a joyful sense of accomplishment and sharing among members of the group. This, of course, is asking a great deal from a pastor. It requires prayer, study, practice, gaining insights from others and a willingness to share the leadership role with other members of the staff, council and parish groups.

We also stressed to the prospective pastors that they should not give up their role as leaders and become laissez-faire. The most successful pastors are those who overcome the temptation to "be in charge" and "call the shots." Neither do they go to the other extreme of giving up their leadership prerogative and handing over their position to others. Rather, they are able to generate a tone of partnership so that all those in leadership positions contribute their wisdom, insight, initiative and ingenuity for the good of the parish community. The pastor is still an essential ingredient in a modern parish, as bearer of the people's dream and as instigator of change to challenge people's complacency and reluctance to respond to the gospels.

Prospective Pastors: Afternoon Session

The afternoon was planned to allow the newly appointed pastors to analyze their parish reports with the diocesan committee contact person who had worked with each transition team.

This was the time for putting flesh on the reports and for discovering aspects and issues about the parish not included in the reports.

The next task was to consider their new staff and council, the transition team and the parish, and to ask themselves what were some of their expectations, negotiables, nonnegotiables, desires and wants as they took on this new pastorate, as well as how this fit the concrete parish reality that lay ahead of them.

They were then given some possible options for their welcoming ritual and had a chance to share ideas with one another about how they would deal with the first few weeks and months of their pastorate. Since the transition teams were an unknown quantity for the new pastors, we spent time exploring the transition team's role in assisting the new pastor. Members of the group offered suggestions to one another for working well with the teams.

We would not meet with these new pastors for another four months, but we felt that they had received the necessary information, tools and motivation to make wise decisions and to avoid most of the common pitfalls associated with assuming new pastorates. For the most part, our instincts proved correct!

Second Workshop Agenda for Outgoing Pastors
(9:30 a.m. to 12:00 p.m.)

Rebonding

Prayer (in my house there are many mansions)

Review of highlights from the January workshop

History line of the last six months (probably not a straight line)

Telling the story: evaluating what worked and didn't work, and why

Break

What to tell the new, incoming pastor (and perhaps what can't be told)

What next? Where to look for new life?

Closing Prayer: A litany of gratitude

Memo to the New Pastor from the Outgoing Pastor

1. Here are a few things I think you need to be aware of as you come to this parish:

About liturgy:

About the folks:

About the staff:

About some possible pitfalls that await you:

2. And here are some things I can't tell you but wish that there was a way for you to find them out:

3. This is my prayer for you:

An Evaluation of the Process for Outgoing Pastors

1. What was helpful? How and why was it helpful?

2. What was not helpful and why?

3. Have you brought things to closure for yourself? For the staff? For the parish? Explain.

4. Do you feel equipped to get on with life? In what ways?

5. Did you help the staff and parish so they feel equipped to get on with life? How?

6. What more could we have done for you? For your staff? For your parish?

7. If this program were to continue, what would you

keep?

change?

add?

Second Workshop Agenda for Parish Transition Teams
(7:30 p.m. to 9:30 p.m.)

SESSION ONE

Rebonding after six months

Prayer

Review of highlights from the January workshop

History line of the last six months (probably not a straight line)

Telling the story: Evaluating what worked and didn't work, and why

Break

Overview of the reports: Filling in the gaps and between the lines

Personal Reflection for later: What are your hopes and concerns for the new pastorate?

Closing Prayer

SESSION TWO

Rebonding

Prayer ritual listing hopes and concerns

Planning a prayer ritual for leadership and the weekend Masses

Presentation on feedback skills needed in dialogue with new pastor

Planning the next six months: History Line
Prayer Ritual
Welcoming
Team Sessions with new pastor

Closing prayer and commitment

A Gathering Prayer

LEADER: Gather us in your love.

ALL: Guide and encourage us!

LEADER: Gather us in your love.

ALL: Let us be open to hear your word!

LEADER: Gather us in your love.

ALL: Comfort us with the wisdom of your Spirit!

LEADER: Let us pray:

ALL: God of love and compassion, open our minds and hearts to your will for us. Let us dream dreams and make choices that will be life-giving for us and for your people. Amen.

READER: Dreams come and dreams go in our lives. Far more die than come to reality. Why is it that we ignore visions that could create new and beautiful worlds? Why do we let ourselves conform and be satisfied with what is?

ALL: Do not let your hearts be troubled. Trust! Even now I am preparing a place for you.

READER: Reaching out to a dream can be risky. It can involve hardships. Our comfortableness can be disturbed. Our lives can seem less secure.

ALL: Do not let your hearts be troubled. Trust! Even now I am preparing a place for you.

READER: Nothing is impossible if we put aside our careful ways. If we build dreams with faith, faith in ourselves, faith in each other, faith in God.

ALL: Do not let your hearts be troubled. Trust! Even now I am preparing a place for you.

SILENT REFLECTION

LEADER: Let us pray:

ALL: Our Father . . .

LEADER: Send your Spirit among us.

ALL: That we may grow in wisdom and understanding.

A Prayerful Homework Assignment for the Transition Teams

List three *hopes* you have for the parish with this new pastor.

1.

2.

3.

List three *concerns* you have as the parish adjusts to the new pastorate.

1.

2.

3.

The Art of Giving Feedback: Note Taker's Outline

Feedback can be both *positive* and *negative.*

It is usually more helpful to give the positive feedback first.

The *motive* for giving feedback will determine how useful the feedback will be.

The *amount* of feedback given in a single session should be limited to how much the recipient can hear.

Timing and location are critical if feedback is to be accepted gracefully.

Feedback should name the *behavior observed.* The person receiving the feedback should always have an opportunity to respond.

Ongoing *support* should follow in whatever ways seem most helpful to the person receiving the feedback.

Feedback Skills for the Transition Teams

Feedback is providing communication to a person (or group) that gives that person (or group) information about how he or she affects others. Feedback gives an individual the chance to consider and then alter behaviors in order to achieve goals more efficiently.

There are eight criteria for providing useful feedback. As you reflect on these criteria, consider how you give feedback as well as what your experience of receiving feedback has been.

1. Useful feedback is *descriptive* rather than evaluative. It describes the sender's reaction, thus leaving the receiver free to use it or not. By avoiding evaluative language, it reduces the need for the receiver to respond defensively.

2. It is *specific* rather than general. It describes the behavior, not the trait.

3. Its motivation is the *growth* of the receiver, not the satisfaction of the giver. Feedback can be destructive when it serves only the giver's needs.

4. It is directed toward behavior that the receiver *can change*. Frustration is only increased when one is reminded of a shortcoming over which one has no control.

5. It is *solicited* rather than imposed. Feedback is most useful when the receiver asks for assistance.

6. It is *well timed*. In general, feedback is most useful when given as soon as possible after the observed behavior.

7. It is checked with the sender. The receiver should be encouraged to rephrase the feedback to ensure clear communication.

8. In a group setting, it is *checked with the group* to discover if it is only one person's perception or if it is shared by others.

New and Prospective Pastors Second Workshop Agenda
(9:30 a.m. to 12:00 p.m.)

SESSION ONE (9:30 a.m. to 12:00 p.m.)

(For the total group of new and prospective pastors)

Rebonding

Prayer

Review stages of transition and where people are at the moment

Individual history lines for last six months
>What's been done?
>What's unfinished?

Sharing the story
>Reactions and reflections
>Where is there disappointment?
>Where is there growth and learning?

Presentation on leadership and collaboration

Closing prayer (lunch break)

SESSION TWO (1:00 p.m. to 3:00 p.m.)

(Only for those new pastors assigned to project parishes)

Analyzing the parish reports

Discussing absolutes, expectations, negotiables, desires

Planning the welcoming ritual: possible options

Sharing ideas from the transition team regarding rituals and results

Suggestions for working with the transition teams

Closing prayer

To an Incoming Pastor We Say, *Do . . .*

1. Preside at parish liturgies in a way that makes people feel welcomed, prayerful and challenged by God's Word.

2. Guide the parish community on its journey of faith by pointing the direction, paying attention to the inspiration of the Spirit and leading people back to the right path when they get off track.

3. Facilitate the running of the parish, not by making all the final decisions but by providing the opportunity for parish leaders to work together on common goals and priorities.

4. Ratify the decisions of the staff and council to give their programs and plans for the parish legitimacy and support.

5. Delegate parish responsibilities to others, leaving yourself free to be the spiritual leader of the people instead of administrating the physical or financial needs of the parish.

6. Set the tone for renewal, spiritual growth and shared leadership in the parish, not by direct action so much as by encouraging others to work toward these ends in the parish.

7. Provide a two-way link between the diocese and parish community, both as the representative of the bishop in the local area and as the voice of the people to the diocese and larger Church.

8. Challenge the people to live out the gospel, especially in areas that may not be getting enough emphasis, such as service to the poor or issues of social justice.

9. Uphold the teachings of the Church so that people are kept informed of and given guidance on moral issues.

10. Be present to the people at key moments in the life of the parish community, both joyful and painful, so that they realize you are with them in good times and bad.

To An Incoming Pastor, We Say, *Don't* . . .

1. Be the boss or sole owner of the parish. Instead, share the responsibility and burden of pastoral leadership with others.

2. Be the doer of all that needs to be done, especially if people fail to show up as promised. It is better to allow a program or activity to fail than to rush in to fill the vacuum.

3. Be the only decision maker. Let others influence and change your opinion. It may turn out to be a better decision in the long run.

4. Be laissez-faire and give up all responsibility as pastor of the parish. Being a strong leader does not mean taking over total control of the parish. Being a strong but nondomineering pastor means accepting the role as guide and instigator of spiritual growth and renewal for the parish community, a task accomplished by working with other parish leaders for the benefit of the parish.

Reflection Sheet for New Pastors

Indicate you preferences for each category in working with the new staff, council, transition team and parish.

ABSOLUTES   *EXPECTATIONS*

NEGOTIABLES   *DESIRES/WANTS*

Chapter Six

May I Have This Dance?

The title of this chapter comes from the name of a book by Joyce Rupp (Notre Dame: Ave Maria Press, 1992). It describes well the mood of the pastors and the parishes as we came to the end of the transition year. Sometime between July and September, a new pastor was installed in each parish. The old song was changed to a new one. The pastor was now asking the leaders and the people, "May I have this dance? Can we make music together? Can we learn to flow with the new rhythm without stepping on each other's toes?"

To help pastor and parish into a new partnership, we met toward the end of October or early November with both the new pastors and the transition teams in each of the three dioceses.

Transition Teams' First Evening

The first gathering in the third phase of the transition process was an evening session with the parish transition teams. The mood of the groups was mixed. Some were pleased with the selection process and were ready to accept the new pastorate. Others were more reserved, waiting to see what would develop.

We began with a prayer centered on the autumn experience of trees turning colors, losing their leaves and preparing for winter. We asked people to become these trees that were undergoing transition. They were to reflect on what is rooted in the soil that endures through change, on the leaves that turn brilliant colors just before they let go and fall to the ground and on the hidden buds that lie dormant waiting to come to life next spring. The autumn trees mirror the Paschal mystery of life, death and resurrection, a journey all of the parishes had been experiencing.

After prayer, we invited each transition team to tell their story of the interim period and the welcoming of the new pastor. Before the whole group, each parish filled in the details of their history line since the last time we had met together in June. One team told of a visit by the prospective pastor to one of the Masses. He wanted to see what it was like and whether it appealed to him. He came as a regular parishioner, hoping not to be recognized. By the end of Mass he was spotted and rumors circulated that he could be their new pastor. To his surprise, he was warmly welcomed as he left the church.

Another team told of closing up the suitcase that had been on the presidential chair during the interim between pastors. A representative of the transition team took the suitcase out of the sanctuary as the new pastor came down the aisle. A third spoke of regular breakfast meetings between a few members of the transition team and the new pastor during the first months of his pastorate in order to ease the adjustment and to talk over ways that would help the pastor feel welcomed.

We asked permission of the transition teams to share these history lines with the new pastors at the next evening's joint session of the teams and the new pastors. All agreed. They were looking forward to discovering what impressions the pastors had of the first few months in the parish.

Realizing that people might not feel free to share with the entire group some of the more difficult aspects of the transition to a new pastor, we asked people to find a partner from another parish and to share those experiences of the recent months that were not so positive or caused stress. The outcome of this sharing revealed that not all aspects of transition are easy. For some, new ways of presiding at liturgy, different approaches to decision making, varied lifestyles and unexpected budget requests had been noticed by parishioners and were relayed to the transition teams. Much as the new pastors had pledged not to come in and make changes in the first six months, the tone and style of the previous pastor was different from the new one. Without making a single concrete change, the transition teams became aware that the parish was already a new reality with the change in leadership.

This insight led to individual reflection on what are hints or hunches, hopes or hindrances that lie ahead in various areas of parish life. We focused on the weekend liturgies, the educational programs, finances and physical plant changes, how decisions will be made, as well as other issues related to staffing and lay leadership.

One team acknowledged that their new pastor liked to sing. This led the team to speculate that the liturgies would have a more joyful, musical aspect in the years ahead. This was a departure from the former pastor for whom music was not a priority. Another team thought that needed repairs to the buildings would now be made because the pastor seemed to be the type of person who got things done. "Our pastor seems to be more of a doer," one person remarked, "than a dreamer as we had in the past."

The participants had no trouble coming up with hints about future emphases and directions for the parish even though their pastors had been in the parish for only a short time. They could identify a new tone and a shift taking place based on the style and inclinations of the new pastor. As the evening came to a close, each team was to pay attention to the new tone and style they had detected in the parish as a result of the change in pastors. They were asked to bring to the next evening's meeting any aspects of the new tone they would like to suggest to the new pastor that he emphasize or foster, as well as any aspects they felt he should perhaps redirect or nuance.

The transition teams were also given a homework assignment for the next evening that included reflection questions about what had been life giving to them personally about this year of transition and what they observed had been life giving to the parish. Were there any aspects of the process that were difficult or frustrating? They were also asked what they had learned over the year about themselves, about their parish, and about the Church in general. We told them that the results of their personal reflection would form the basis for the evaluation piece of the next evening's session.

It was not easy for the transition teams to give up two evenings in the week for these sessions. But they admitted that this interval between sessions did give them a chance to mull over what was happening in the transition process and added to the richness of the experience. One diocese chose to have only one extended evening session for the transition teams. While it was possible to accomplish the required tasks in a single 5:00 p.m. to 9:30 p.m. session, we became aware of what was lost in this model of one rather than two evening sessions for the transition teams. The most obvious loss was the personal reflection and prayer that took place between the two 7:30 p.m. to 9:30 p.m. evening sessions. The added interaction and insight among participants as a result of the "at-home" reflection was noticeably absent in the single evening format.

New Pastors' Workshop

While the transition teams were doing their "at-home" re-flection, the new pastors gathered together for an afternoon session. They, too, had a chance to pray together and to reflect on their entry experience into the parish. Each person constructed a history line of the last four or five months and had the opportunity to share this with the entire group. One pastor entitled the account of this brief journey as "A New Place Called Home." The new pastors went on at length about what the experience had meant to them. Putting limits on their sharing was difficult. One person remarked that he never had a chance to tell his story about his transitions before this one. This time was going to be different. He came ready and willing to tell his story, primarily because it was so much more positive than previous changes.

Another pastor talked in glowing terms about arriving in the parish amid signs and salutations from the transition team, the staff and council members. This combined welcoming committee was especially solicitous about his needs and desires for his living space. The previous pastor, a member of a religious order, had lived a Spartan existence, which fit him but may not fit the new pastor. Within a few days the new pastor made up a list of needs, including new kitchen utensils, a rug for the living room, bigger pillows for the bed, a microwave oven and, partly in jest, a deck off the sitting room.

The leaders were delighted with the list and set off to make good on his requests. They knew he was kidding about the deck, but they seized on this as their new project. They quickly enlisted talent from the parish, made up a plan to the pastor's liking, and within a month, had the new deck completed. The pastor was amazed by their enthusiasm and generosity. It was something he had never experienced in any previous parish. The parishioners were so delighted by the results of their labors and the obvious pleasure of the pastor that they held the official welcoming reception on the lawn surrounding the new deck. The only concern the pastor had was whether the new deck would support all the people and food that filled it at his welcoming party. He shared this story with the other pastors amid laughter and shouts of approval by the other new pastors.

Another pastor's experience was not as positive. He had planned to take a break between his previous assignment and his new one. He was so excited and anxious about becoming the new pastor that he canceled his plans and showed up at the parish two weeks before anyone expected him to be there. When he arrived, nothing was ready. The rectory was empty. The previous pastor had moved out and nothing had been done since. It was dirty and not fit for habitation. The staff and the transition team had made arrangements for redoing the entire house with new rugs, paint and linens. It was scheduled for next week, but the pastor was here now. It was then he realized he had made a mistake. But he had nowhere else to go. "It was the worst night of my life," he said. "Now I know the benefit of an interval between assignments. It is not just for me. It's meant for the parish as well. I learned my lesson the hard way."

After the new pastors had all shared their four-month history line, we asked whether they would be willing to share them with their transition team that evening, along with the stories they shared with one another. To a person they said they would. They also wanted to see what the transition team's history line of the same period looked like.

The new pastors were then asked to name the new reality they walked into. We asked each person to fill out a reflection sheet that compared what they *expected* they would get when they accepted the assignment with what the actual situation was like. The areas of comparison included the staff, the lay leaders, such as the council and coordinating committees or commissions, the parishioners and their own living situation. Even though the pastors had been in place only a short time, they could already identify the differences between their dreams and the reality.

One pastor spoke of being confronted in the first month of his pastorate with a conflict over Masses held in the school gym and those in the main church. Because of a cutback in the number of priests, he could not honor both commitments. Eliminating Masses, however, would cause a serious rift in the parish. This was something that the outgoing pastor was supposed to have handled but had not. Now he was saddled with this sticky issue and a decision had to be made quickly because he, for one, had not figured out how to preside at two simultaneous liturgies in different locations. He had no idea that the matter had not been dealt with as promised before his arrival.

Another pastor spoke of friction between himself and one of the staff members. He got off on the wrong foot because of an idle comment he made about balanced language in the liturgy that caused the staff member "to go ballistic," as he described it. At the moment he was "back-pedaling like mad but staying in the same place, like an exercise bike."

These descriptions of the contrast between the dream and the reality were helpful to the new pastors. They listened respectfully to each other, giving each other support and, where appropriate, personal insights. The stories reinforced their own experience that every transition has disappointments and pitfalls, as well as joys and triumphs. This sharing was followed by an exercise that had been done the previous evening with the transition teams. We asked the new pastors to fill out a work sheet concerning the hints or hunches they had about what is likely to happen in key areas of the parish over the course of their pastorate.

For instance, in worship, one pastor had the hunch that he would not be able to go as fast as he had hoped in making changes in the liturgy and bringing in recommendations from the diocesan liturgy office. "The people have had so little experience of what the liturgies could or should be," he remarked. "I do not sense resistance so much as blank stares and lack of any response or reaction. I'm going to have to go pretty slowly with any new approaches. Eventually they will come around but we'll have to do it together. If it's just my thing, I think I'll lose them."

In education, one pastor complained about a heavy school emphasis in his new parish. "Everything revolves around the school and it is where most of the money is spent. I hope we can start shifting some of the focus to formation in the parish as a whole and integrate the school community into the parish without alienating the parents."

Parish finances was another area in which the pastors were asked to identify hints about future trends and directions. One pastor said he uncovered a few "secret" accounts belonging to some of the long-standing organizations of the parish. "I'm going to step on some toes, I know," he said, "but the finances will have to be handled with more accountability and disclosure. We might even have a change in the makeup of the finance board. Some of its members have been on it for years."

When asked what lies ahead in maintaining the parish buildings, one pastor said with a shrug, "I don't look forward to it, but I'm afraid we are going to have to build a new parish center. Not a pleasant thought. I just came from a building drive in the last parish and I was looking forward to not having to do *that* again. No such luck, but the people seem happy that I was named pastor just because of my previous experience with fund-raising and designing buildings. It's not an expertise I value very highly, I'm afraid."

One pastor had the feeling that in five to ten years the area around the parish might be undergoing an ethnic and racial shift. "I'm wondering if my special ministry will be to help the people through this transition while still maintaining our high level of community and involvement. We had better prepare for it now rather than be surprised by the shift and let it dictate to us what the parish will become rather than the other way around. It will be a test for us of Christian hospitality and inclusiveness. It may also be a great gift to the parish if we prepare now to meet this challenge."

Styles of Pastoring

These stories about what the pastors might be facing in the months and years ahead led to a discussion of Robert Dale's three aspects of leadership styles. (See *Pastoral Leadership*, Nashville: Abingdon Press, 1986.) Dale suggests that a successful pastorate depends on the proper balance of the pastor's leadership style, the people's desires and expectations, and the environment within which the pastor's and people's interaction takes place. Dale offers four combinations of these elements that work well:

LEADER	PEOPLE	ENVIRONMENT
Commander	Dependent	Unstable – overly stable
Encourager	Receiver	Orderly
Hermit	Self-starter	Self-sustaining
Catalyst	Participant	Cooperation

One leadership style is similar to a *commander* of an army or a captain on a boat. There is one person in charge, the pastor, and he is the one calling the shots and giving the orders. The way in which the orders are given can cover a wide range of approaches, from dictatorial to benevolent, but there is no doubt who is commanding the ship.

This leadership style works well in a parish where the predominant attitude among staff, leaders and people is one of dependency. They are perfectly willing to have the pastor make the final decisions. It saves a great deal of time in discussion; it is efficient and uncomplicated. This attitude in parishes where the previous pastor was a commander and trained the people to expect this style, or when the previous pastor was nondirective and laissez-faire. A parish that lacks direction may welcome with open arms a new pastor who arrives with a decisive manner of decision making. "Finally we have someone who knows how to make decisions and give us some direction," they exclaim.

The parish environment that reinforces a commanding style of pastoring is either highly unstable or overly stable and predictable. In the latter case, if people are used to the pastor making all important decisions, then they will be happy when one commander is replaced by another. In the former case, where the environment is full of confusion and ambiguity and the ship seems to have lost its rudder, then this climate supports a commanding style of pastoring as well.

A second configuration of leadership that is successful is one in which the pastor exhibits an *encouraging* type of leading. He is always present to the people, both before and after the Masses, during coffee and donuts, at parish gatherings. He is like the ideal hospital chaplain with an excellent bedside manner. He listens well to people's stories and he has a steady repertoire of his own to share with others. This type of pastoring thrives on social interaction and is a great builder of community spirit.

This approach to pastoring works if the people are willing to be receivers of this pastoral style of encourager. Setting goals, taking action and following a pastoral plan are not emphasized in this model of pastoring. Someone else will have to take care of the details of running a parish. The tone set by the pastor is friendliness, acceptance and hospitality. This interaction of an encouraging pastor and receiv-

ing parishioners will work if the predominant environment
is orderly and free of conflict or crisis. The parish must be
on an even keel, with bills paid, buildings in good shape and
a stable population. Then both pastor and people are free
to enjoy each other's company, to grow in mutual love and
care for each other and to set an example of Christian charity
to all that come in contact with the community. Returning
to the model of a chaplain with a good bedside manner, this
style is successful if all the cares and concerns related to
running a hospital or nursing home are taken care of, and
the priest is free to minister to the spiritual and human needs
of the patient.

A third combination of pastor, people and environment doesn't sound like a leadership style, but in a way it is.
It frees people to be creative and take initiative, which is a
great gift in a leader, given the right situation. Robert Dale
calls this type of leading a *hermit* style. The pastor pulls back
and lets the people "run with it." There is still a visible,
recognizable leader, but the pastor's role is not to make
decisions or give direction. In some places this is a conscious
choice so that people will assume more leadership and
ownership of the parish. In other places it is more by default
because the pastor is unable or unwilling to take an active
role in leading the parish. This may come as a result of
sickness or because he does not feel up to the task.

Whatever the reason, a hermit style of pastoring works
if a sufficient number of the parishioners are self-starters.
They thrive when given the chance to make decisions and
set direction, to formulate goals and action plans and to see
results. The parish can flourish in this climate so long as the
overall environment is self-sustaining. Because the pastor
has blessed the efforts of any and all groups and individuals
to take initiative, there is usually no common plan or direction. Many activities and programs will be acting on their
own, each doing good ministry, but not tied together or
sharing a common vision. For that reason, the parish must
be able to maintain itself in the midst of this varied activity
and multiple functioning. If the parish is well-structured and
people are kept in touch with what all the groups are doing,

then the initiatives of the self-starters can be maintained and encouraged. The pastor's role in this situation is to be the legitimator and figurehead, blessing all the activity that is taking place but not having much influence on what is happening.

As the new pastors discussed each of the three configurations of leadership, they realized that all have benefits as well as liabilities. The commander style of pastoring is efficient, but it also fosters passive parishioners and alienates the people who want a more participative style of decision making. The encourager style creates a good sense of community and camaraderie, but what is gained in friendliness is lost in not providing direction or a sense of mission to the parish. The hermit style is not as bad as it seems at first glance. It does foster ownership, and it gets people involved on all levels of parish leadership and ministry. But it suffers from a lack of focus and a common vision. Having everyone going off in different directions is not always the best model of pastoral leadership. People feel insecure if the one who is supposed to be the pastor has "abdicated the throne," as they put it.

The discussion led to a fourth style of pastoring that we held up as the most desirable model and the one that had the best chance of succeeding in a modern parish context. In this configuration, the pastor acts as a *catalyst*. The leader's role is to create the framework or the occasion for people to come together and decide what the direction and future of the parish might be. With the staff, the catalyst pastor creates an atmosphere of mutual trust and partnership. On the council and in other coordinating groups, the catalyst sparks interest and motivates people to share the leadership role and decision making of the parish. The tone is not *advising* the pastor but *joining* the pastor in a common cause.

The catalyst style only succeeds if the people, whether staff, leaders or parishioners, are willing to be participants in this call to be coworkers and partners in leadership. The environment must be cooperative, with no backbiting, hidden agendas or passive-aggressive behavior. One pastor talked about coming into a previous assignment, hoping to act as a catalyst only to find it failing miserably. Only now did he realize that he had walked into a community that was waiting for him to make decisions. That is what they were use to. When he failed to do this, they became hostile and uncooperative, bucking him at every turn. There is more to leadership, in other words, than just the pastor. It is a mixture of leader, people and environment. If these three are not in sync, then no matter what the pastor may desire, it will never happen. The discussion of leadership concluded with ways in which a catalyst style might be fostered in a parish, given each person's type of community and environment.

Before bringing the new pastor's workshop to a close, one last aspect of pastoring was addressed, that of self-care. Who is going to save the lifeguard? As the shortage of priests grows more acute, special care must be given to maintaining realistic workloads and establishing healthy interests and pursuits outside the ministry. As a help in this regard, each person was given a work sheet on what might be a reasonable workload for them. Identifying a norm, a common baseline, a maximum limit to pastoral duties was not an easy task. "How can I limit my hours," one priest asked, "if the people need me?"

This led to a wonderfully rich discussion of alternatives and options. They recognized that limits had to be placed on the number of Masses each weekend, including weddings and funerals, the number of hours spent in extraparochial activities each week, either in the diocese or elsewhere, the number of evening meetings attended. The pastors even discussed what would be the ideal distance between home and workplace. Does "living over the store" always lead to better ministry?

The session concluded with questions that each pastor was to reflect on and come prepared to present at the combined session with the transition teams that evening. The questions for reflection including the following:

What do you want to affirm that is now going on in the parish?

What challenges do you think you will be facing?

What aspects of the parish do you want to emphasize or focus on in the near future?

What will you have to let go of as you assume this new pastorate?

The gathering of new pastors ended as it had begun, in prayer and personal reflection. Only an hour separated this session and the dinner celebration that would be the start of the next combined session with the new pastors and transition teams.

Pastors and Teams Together

The combined session began with a celebrative meal and a chance for all the transition teams and new pastors to meet each other and share stories. Spirits were high as the process drew to a close.

After the meal, each parish assembled around a table that included the pastor, the transition team members and the diocesan contact person. The opening prayer was based on the the scripture story of putting new wine into new wineskins. The parishes were beginning a new era, a new journey of faith with new leadership. Old ways must give way to new, not denying the benefits of the old but not trying to recapture them either.

What followed was a night of storytelling and assessing future directions. The pastors and the transition teams shared each other's history lines of the previous six months. One pastor told his transition team that he was not really thinking about coming to their parish, but when he saw their report and came to visit the parish, he realized it would be a good fit after all. It was only then that he gave his name to the personnel board as a possible candidate. Another pastor talked about his concern in applying for the parish because he wasn't sure he had what it would take to be their pastor.

It was the interim period workshop for prospective pastors that gave him the confidence to apply. He came to realize that leading the parish was not all *his* responsibility. He was not the only dreamer of what the parish could be in the future. He had to trust the gifts of staff and lay leaders and learn to share the load. The transition team was delighted to hear this and gave him support and affirmation in making the choice to become their new pastor.

The comparison of time lines was revealing to pastors and teams alike. The perspectives and emphases of each were different. The teams stressed their anxiousness in wanting to make the pastor feel welcome and to help ease the transition period. The pastors talked more about fitting into a new home, letting go of the previous community of friends, adjusting to a new staff and trying to remember names and getting to know people.

The pastors and teams also shared their hints and hunches about the future that each worked on at the previous sessions. These, too, were enlightening to the group. Each came with a unique perspective of what might lie ahead for the parish. The pastors were trying not to make any sudden, big changes. The transition teams were aware of changes that had already taken place that the pastors had missed or had taken for granted: subtle changes in liturgical styles, availability and approachableness of the pastor, ways of organizing staff and council meetings, nuances in lifestyle and personal preferences. None of these were radical shifts, but they did make a difference. The pastors listened with rapt attention, becoming more and more appreciative of how much the transition teams had noticed in such a short time, or how much they themselves revealed about their own styles and ways of operating.

The interchange was interrupted by frequent bursts of laughter as both pastors and teams from each parish shared insights about the initial months of the new pastorate. They remarked afterward how much they enjoyed the frank and honest sharing among pastors and people. One outcome of the sharing was a commitment by one parish to hold open meetings so that more people could talk with the pastor about these issues. They planned a few town halls, similar to those held in the first stages of the transition process, to allow a wider group discussion about changes people had noticed in the parish thus far and what they saw as new directions or emphases in the future. Another parish picked up on the idea and started planning their parish gatherings. One team came up with a name for the event, "Come rap with Father Ray."

This sharing of history lines and hints about the future in parish groups was followed by a presentation by each new pastor to the whole group. Between their afternoon session and the dinner, they reflected on questions related to their pastoring role in the parish. They now had a chance to share their reflections with one another and with the transition teams.

The first area was on what the pastors wanted to affirm in the parish. A few of the pastors succeeded priests who had been in the parish for a number of years, while others followed pastors for whom this was their last assignment before retirement. The new pastors talked about wanting to be sensitive to this long tradition and felt no need to change the general direction of the parish. One pastor joked about the street outside the church that had been renamed in honor of the pastor who had retired. "If ever I forget to affirm all the good that went on before I came, I have only to look out the window at that street sign to remind me." Other pastors talked about deciding to choose the parish because of all the good that is going on. "All I want to do," one remarked, "is not get in the way of its continuing."

The second question was on the challenges facing the new pastors. Some of the pastors mentioned immediate crises that had to be dealt with, such as reducing the number of Masses because of one less priest or having to find ways of paying the school teachers' salaries in the midst of deficit spending. One of the new pastors was not a priest but a nonordained pastoral administrator. His challenge was to allay people's fears that this was the first step toward closing the parish. As a whole, the people seemed to accept him but the anxiety and uneasiness were not far beneath the surface.

Some of the long-range challenges mentioned included new building projects, keeping the school afloat, not getting overextended with parish demands, figuring out future staffing needs and positions and coping with divergent and vocal factions in the parish.

The third question was on aspects of the parish the pastors might focus on or emphasize in the near future. The transition teams were especially attentive to the responses to this question because they might offer clues about shifts in the next year or two. The pastors seemed aware of this and assured the gathering that they were not there to make the parish into their own image and likeness. At the same time, they all talked about parts of the parish that gave them energy and got their juices going. For one, this was the weekend liturgies. He felt more could be done to give them life and spark. For another, it was young adults, whom he considered to be a "sleeping giant" in the parish. For a third, it was fostering small groups. Although a few groups had kept meeting since Renew was in the parish, it was not encouraged or brought into the mainstream of the parish as well as it might be, was his observation.

The teams were delighted to hear these reflections and the pastors themselves gained insights from one another. Next it was the transition teams' turn to shine. They had been given homework the night before that asked them to reflect on what had been life giving to them personally and the parish during the year-long process, as well as areas that had been difficult.

Almost to a person, the team members talked of how much they had learned about the parish itself and about the importance of helping it through transition issues. They spoke of being grateful to be selected for this task. Despite the hard work it involved, they said they gained much more than they gave. The joyful spirit surrounding the evening's interaction was proof of this.

Some of the highlights included having the chance to work with other parish teams in the midst of transition. This kept the work in focus and helped them realize that they were not alone in the struggles they faced. Others said that the parishioners came to believe that their opinions and insights did make a difference. Although many questioned this at the outset, they came to realize that the diocese did pay attention to the parish reports and that the new pastors were influenced in their choices because of this information from the parishes.

Some of the difficulties stemmed from not knowing what was happening to all the information supplied by the transition teams to the diocese. This was what made the interim period so frustrating. Would we get a pastor soon? Is anyone interested in applying for our parish? Will we get someone who fits our needs and situation? These were the questions who were on people's minds during the period of unknowing. At the same time, the teams were happy to be the first to journey through this pilot process. They saw the benefits it had over the traditional model of one pastor leaving and the next showing up the next day with little or no input from leaders and people. Each participant of this process, pastors and teams alike, was asked to fill out an evaluation sheet following the final session. Reflections on these evaluations are included in the final chapter of this book.

Before this combined session of pastors and teams came to an end, one final piece of business remained. How and when would the transition teams put closure to their work and identity as a group? They were called together in January as a temporary commitment. Their work had now come to an end. How would they celebrate the conclusion of their task?

It was different for each group. A few decided that this evening's session would be a fitting close for them. They had done their work. Nothing more was required of them. The final prayer wishing everyone good-bye would be their closure. Others, after some urging from their new pastors, decided to have a more formal closing ceremony in the parish. One pastor asked that the team come to one of the weekend Masses as a group to be acknowledged for their work and to attend a small reception after Mass as a way of saying thank-you.

For a few teams, their work had not quite been completed. In one parish, the formal ceremony of welcoming the new pastor had not yet taken place and they wanted to be in on the planning of this special event. For another, no permanent pastor had been assigned, only a temporary priest administrator for one year. The transition was not over for the parish, so they felt committed to staying in place until a permanent pastor was assigned. The variety of times and methods for closure among the transition teams is one more example of how important it is to remain flexible in the transition process. No one model and time line fits all. Each place has its own rhythm and deadlines.

The evening finished with the following reading from St. Paul's first letter to the Thessalonians. All felt it summed up well the experience they had of a change in pastor.

> Live together in peace, and our instruction to this end is to reprimand the unruly, encourage the timid, help the weak and be patient with all men and women. Be sure that no one repays a bad turn with a bad turn; good should be your objective always, among yourselves and in the world at large. Be happy in your faith at all times. Never stop praying. Be thankful whatever the circumstances may be. If you follow this advice you will be working out the will of God expressed to you in Christ Jesus. Never damp the fire of the Spirit, and never despise what is spoken in the name of God. By all means, use your judgment, and hold on to whatever is really good. Steer clear of evil in any form. And may the God of peace make you holy and happy through and through.
>
> 1 Thess. 5:14-23.
> Adapted from J. B. Phillips,
> *The New Testament in Modern English*
> (New York: Macmillan, 1962)

New Pastors Third Workshop Agenda
(2:00 p.m. to 6:00 p.m.)

Introduction

Prayer

The transition experience: A new place called home

Naming the new reality: So what did you expect?
                        Staff, leadership, parishioners,
                        living situation

Hints about the future:
        Liturgy
        Education
        Finances
        Physical plant
        Decision making
        Environment

Break

Your role and style as pastor
        Previous experience
        Gifts and talents
        Hopes and inclinations

Exploring the pastoral role:
        The changing face of parish and pastor
        A reasonable workload

Relating to the transition team
        Their role and bringing it to closure

An Autumn Prayer

No new growth will come unless autumn agrees to let go of what has been. The same is true of our lives.

Consider an autumn tree. Let the tree symbolize yourself. For each part of the tree reflect on the following questions:

The roots: who and what has been your nourishment and vitality? Who and what roots you in this time of significant change?

The trunk: what events have channeled new life into you and at this time of transition?

The leaves: what is dying in your life now? What do you feel called to let go of?

The bark: who or what protects you? Comforts you?

The terminal buds: what is waiting to bud into new life?

A Time for Sharing

AND SO WE PRAY:

God of the seasons, there is a time for everything: there is a time for dying, a time for rising. Give us the courage to enter into this transformation process, we pray:

LET US PRAY TO OUR GOD.

God of autumn, the trees are saying good-bye to their green, letting go of what has been. We, too, have our moments of surrender, with all their insecurity and risk. Help us to let go of all that we need to, we pray:

LET US PRAY TO OUR GOD.

God of fallen leaves lying in colored patterns on the ground, our lives have their own patterns. Let us learn from the patterns of our lives, we pray:

LET US PRAY TO OUR GOD.

God of the harvest, many gifts lie within the season of our surrender. We must wait for the harvest in faith and hope. That we may have patience when we do not recognize the patterns, we pray:

LET US PRAY TO OUR GOD.

God of geese going south for another season, your wisdom enables us to know what needs to be left behind and what needs to be carried into the future. Share with us your insight and wisdom, we pray:

LET US PRAY TO OUR GOD.

God of flowers touched with frost, may your love keep our hearts from growing cold in the empty season, we pray:

LET US PRAY TO OUR GOD.

God of life you believe in us, you enrich us, you entrust us with the freedom to choose life. Grace us with grateful hearts, we pray:

LET US PRAY TO OUR GOD.

LET US PRAY:

God of love, you enter into our autumn seasons, into our deepest places of inner dwelling, into our times of transition. May we allow the experiences of autumn to speak to us of necessary change and growth. Grant us an openness to the continuous process of letting go and moving on, which is part of the human condition. We are grateful that you are a faithful companion on this journey. Amen.

Adapted from Joyce Rupp's *May I Have This Dance?*

A Reflection Sheet for New Pastors

YOUR DREAM	THE REALITY

1. Staff:

2. Leaders (council, committees, groups):

3. Parishioners:

4. Living situation:

A Reflection on What Lies Ahead
Insights, Hunches, Roadblocks, Hopes, Fears, Possibilities

1. Weekend liturgies:

2. Educational programs, children and adults:

3. Finances, income and expenses:

4. Physical plant, present condition and expansion:

5. Decision making and power issues:

6. The surrounding area and local environment:

A Reasonable Workload for Pastors

1. Number of hours you are available in your ministry each week   _____

2. Number of hours away from your duties each week

     _____

3. Number of weeks for vacation each year (includes Sundays)   _____

4. Number of days for retreat each year   _____

5. Distance between your home and the workplace

     _____

6. Number of hours in diocesan or extraparochial responsibilities per month (part of the total hours listed in 1 above)   _____

7. Number of professional enrichment days per year

     _____

8. Six months sabbatical every (number of years)

     _____

9. Number of scheduled Masses per weekend at which you preside   _____

10. Number of liturgical celebrations per weekend that you lead (weddings, baptisms, etc.)   _____

11. Number of reconciliation sessions per week

     _____

12. Number of scheduled Masses per weekday at which you preside   _____

Pastor's Presentation to the Transition Teams on His Role as the New Pastor

1. What do you want to affirm that is now going on in the parish?

2. What challenges do you think you will be facing?

3. What aspects of the parish do you want to emphasize or focus on in the near future?

4. What will you have to let go of as you assume the new pastorate?

Parish Transition Team Third Workshop Agenda

SESSION ONE (7:30 p.m. to 9:30 p.m.)

Rebonding

Prayer

Tell the story of the interim period, the welcoming and feedback to the new pastor. (Come prepared to tell the story to the whole group.)

What more needs to be included?

Hints about the future
    Liturgy
    Education
    Finances
    Physical plant
    Decision making
    Environment

Identifying the new tone: What to nourish and what to redirect

Homework: Reflecting on what this experience has been for us

SESSION TWO (6:30 p.m. [supper] to 9:30 p.m.)

Simple supper of celebration and interaction between teams and pastors

Prayer

Comparing hints about the future from teams and pastors:
    Common and uncommon elements

Pastors' presentation on their role: What to affirm, challenge, emphasize, let go

Parish presentations on what the experience has meant for them

Evaluation of the process and Closing Prayer

For Your Prayerful Consideration: Transition Team Homework

Step 1: Revisit your involvement in this transitioning
process.

Step 2: What has been life giving for you personally?

What has been life giving for the parish?

What has been difficult or frustrating?

Step 3: What have you learned about:

Yourself?

Your parish?

The Church?

Beginning a New Tradition and a New History
Opening Prayer for the Second Session

Nobody tears a piece from a new coat to patch up an old one. If you do, you ruin the new one and the new piece does not match the old.

Nobody puts new wine into old wineskins. If you do, the new wine will burst the skins – the wine will be spilled and the skins, ruined.

No, new wine must be put into new wineskins.

Of course, nobody who has been drinking old wine will want the new at once. The person is sure to say, "The old is a good sound wine."

Luke 5:36-39. Adapted from
J. B. Phillips, *The New Testament in Modern English* (New York: Macmillan, 1962)

An Evaluation

Reflect on the entire process, January to November.

1. What was helpful and why was it helpful?

2. What was not helpful? Why?

3. What more could we have done for you? For your team? For your parish?

4. If this program were to continue, what would you keep?

5. What would you change?

6. What would you add?

7. Add any further comments you think would help us evaluate this process.

Chapter Seven

Could We Do This on Our Own?

Your diocese does not have a well-developed process for the transition of pastors, but your parish is about to go through this change. The current pastor's tenure will come to an end soon, or perhaps he is about to retire, or maybe the pastor feels it is time for a change.

You would like to give this transition the attention it deserves, but you will have to plan it on your own. The diocese may have an open-listing policy whereby priests can apply for a parish that will have a vacant pastorate. It may even have representatives from the priests' personnel board or diocesan placement committee visit the parish to ascertain the unique history, character and needs of your parish. Once they gather the information, they return to their diocesan offices to process the information. You may not hear the outcome of this work until a pastor has been selected. Nor is there an interim between the outgoing pastor and the new one to give both the parish and the new appointee time to catch their breath and make the adjustment.

Is there anything that a parish and its leadership can do to provide for a creative and well-planned transition period? Yes, indeed there is. If the following steps are followed, not only will the parish be doing itself and the changing pastors a favor, it might even offer the diocese a model for a transition process that could be used in other parishes as well. You owe it to yourselves and to the larger Church to give it a try. Difficult as it is to do this process on your own, the benefits for the future of both the parish and the diocese are many.

A word of caution, however. Some parts of the process may not be as successful or as satisfying as when the process is conducted as a diocesan project that has the support of the bishop, the resources of diocesan personnel and the support and interaction of other parishes that are also undergoing a change of pastors. Most likely your parish will not have the benefit of knowing beforehand the pool of prospective pastors and pastoral associates who are themselves in transition and are looking for placement in a parish. Despite these drawbacks, what you can do is create the atmosphere of a well-planned and organized process of transition that will help the outgoing pastor and parishioners prepare for this important moment in their history. This emphasis on the process of transition may also alert those in the diocese (or, as we will address later in this chapter, the religious congregation) that the parish is taking the change in pastors seriously and that the diocese should do the same in order to assure a good match of pastor and people and a smooth changeover of pastoral leadership.

Getting Started

A change in pastors is on the horizon. The ending time has begun. The tenure of the current pastor, or perhaps his retirement, is approaching. Timing is important. It is possible to start the transition process too early. If the transition goes on too long, everyone – priest and people alike – can be exhausted by farewell parties and leave-taking ceremonies. It becomes too much of a good thing. But neither should the transition be done too quickly. People need time to process and reflect on the change, time to grieve and let go, time to accept and embrace the change. Six months from announcement to leave-taking is a good rule of thumb. If June is the time for the pastor's farewell, then the transition process should start in January of the same year.

The first step is to call a joint session of the staff and pastoral council to present the situation. The pastor announces that he will be leaving the parish on June 30. The more the parish can do to prepare for his departure and to present its case for a good replacement to the diocese, the better are its chances for a suitable successor.

This joint session of key pastoral leaders has two functions. One is to suggest names for a transition team that will shepherd the parish through the transition. The second is to map out a time line for the transition process. For the first task, consult chapter 3 for the makeup of the transition team and the responsibilities it will have. We have found it helpful to have a mixture of people on the team, perhaps one staff and one council member, a few active parishioners, a longtime parishioner and a newcomer or two. Telling them the importance of their task and that it will last no more than ten months makes the recruitment of the team easier. The staff member on the team should act as a resource to the group but should not be the chairperson. If this happens, team members tend to acquiesce to "the professional" and not take as much ownership of the task. The pastor, of course, should not be a member of the team.

A sample time line for the process may begin in January by contacting diocesan personnel about what the parish has in mind. This is also the time to form the transition team. In March, the transition team hosts gatherings of the parish leadership and parishioners as a means for preparing a report on the parish that describes its unique character, its strengths and needs, and preferred styles of pastoral leadership that fosters growth and provides continuity in the parish. The team also describes to parishioners, either through announcements or articles, the transition process.

In April and May, the team plans special liturgies and other parish functions centering on "letting go," a time to celebrate the pastor's leadership, allowing people to say good-bye and to grieve the loss. In June or July, the parish has a chance to be "pastor-less." It is to be hoped that the diocese (or religious congregation) respects the desires of the staff and council to not replace the outgoing pastor immediately. Two, three or even four weeks may elapse before the new pastor arrives. This will give both the parish and the new replacement time to adjust.

In July or August the pastor arrives. The team plans the initial welcoming, as well as a formal dedication and commitment ritual. They also plan a special feedback session for staff and council several months into the new pastorate. This allows both pastor and people a chance to share insights and offer suggestions about the future.

This is a sample time line for the transition process. Whether all the components fit this schedule is another matter. A replacement may not be available in time, or the leave-taking may have to be adjusted because of other circumstances. One of the tasks of the transition team is to remain flexible and be ready to make adjustments and adaptations if and when necessary. Its role is to keep the process moving ahead but not in a lockstep fashion.

This sample process is all well and good in an ideal parish, but what about a less-than-ideal situation? What if the current pastor who is facing a change within the year is not open to an extended transition process? He would rather, as one pastor once told us, "just slip out the back door and disappear into the night." "I find it too difficult to say good-bye to people. Better to keep it quiet and surprise them," was his response. In another situation, the pastor may not be well liked, for whatever reason, by some of the parishioners. He is reluctant to undergo a transition process for fear of the negative feedback it might produce. What steps can the staff and council take in these less-than-ideal occasions? For these cases, before a joint gathering of leaders is called, it may be helpful to find one or more persons whom the pastor trusts and admires – people whose wisdom he can consider. They may approach him at an opportune moment and show him the benefits of a transition process – the opportunity this provides for healing and closure. It is the best interest of pastor and parish to spend time saying good-bye to each other. This process will send him forth on a positive footing and will open up the possibilities for a worthy successor. More often than not, this one-on-one, nonthreatening encounter opens the reluctant pastor to seeing the wisdom of this approach and the benefits it offers to both him and the parish.

Saying Good-bye and Preparing the Report

The transition team has two tasks during the first phase of the process: to help the pastor put closure to his term of office and to prepare a report on the special character and unique aspects of the parish. All the materials contained in chapter 4 apply to an individual parish as well. For instance, helping the pastor say good-bye to key groups and individuals, encouraging him to take care of loose ends and unfinished business, planning leave-taking rituals and celebrations, keeping the process before the minds and hearts of the people – all these are the tasks of the transition team in the first phase of its work.

Because the parish is "going it alone," it is also the duty of the transition team to stay in close contact with the diocese, letting key diocesan personnel know what it is doing and why. It would be ideal to have a contact person from the priests' personnel board or diocesan placement office to be the liaison between the parish and the diocese. This would make sure that information flows easily back and forth and that no suspicions or misunderstandings arise between the diocese and parish leaders. The diocesan offices and the bishop himself need to be assured that the parish is not going beyond diocesan policies or in any way wishes to "choose" or even interview prospective pastors. At the same time, the leadership lets the diocese know how important a moment this is in the life and operation of the parish, that it wants to do its best to assure a positive attitude among both priests and parishioners during this time of transition. The team will need to share its time line with the diocese and indicate the reasoning behind each step of the process.

The second task of the team during this first phase is to prepare a report on the parish for diocesan placement personnel. The report should include the items suggested in chapter 4:

What do we as a parish want to hold on to?

What are we willing to let go of?

What new things would we be willing to try out?

What characteristics would we like to see in the new pastor?

What special aspects do we bring to the new position?

What makes us unique and different as a parish?

What is the profile of the parish in terms of size, age, background, programs, liturgies, emphases, goals and future directions?

This information is collected through a series of parish gatherings, beginning with the staff and council, either as separate groups or in a joint session. We recommend that the current pastor not be present at these sessions, but that he have an opportunity to reflect on these questions on his own so that his wisdom and insights can be included in the report.

The leadership session begins with a history line of the present pastorate, all the significant events, whether pluses or minuses, since the present pastor arrived, to the present moment. Following this exercise as a total group, people reflect individually and then in small groups on the questions listed above. The leaders reconvene from the small groups to share their insights and to discover common threads. The results of this discussion are recorded by the transition team for the final report. The team also seeks the help of the staff and council to act as facilitators at the larger parish-wide sessions. These "town halls" follow the same format of history line, individual reflection, small group discussion and large group sharing. The transition team then collates and organizes this information into a concise report of ten to twenty pages. Documents that are longer tend to overwhelm the readers and may not have the impact that the report is supposed to have.

Once the report is completed, by Easter time, it is presented to the diocesan contact person or to the personnel board as a whole. Ideally, this can be done at a joint meeting of the staff and council so they can flesh out the written report and relate personally to diocesan personnel the tone and flavor of the parish gatherings, as well as highlight key aspects and insights in the report.

The next step is prayer. The report is now in the hands of the bishop and diocesan personnel, who will circulate copies to prospective pastors or, in some cases, nonordained pastoral administrators. Parish leaders and the transition team have already made it clear to the diocese that they are open to having any and all possible candidates come and talk to them about the parish in general or about the report in particular. The team also encourages the parish to pray for a suitable successor, asking the parishioners to be aware that the "perfect replacement" does not exist. The people should pray that the Holy Spirit find a person who will be a good match for the parish, one who will fit in well and lead it on its journey of faith.

Sudden Changes

What we have been describing is the ideal scenario: the pastor knows when his tenure is up and the parish can prepare ahead of time for the change. Such preparation is not always possible. If can happen that a pastor dies suddenly or is removed from office with no warning or preparation. As described in chapter 2, during the first stage of transition there is a loss of focus. Everything is changed. It is no longer business as usual. Routine actions become difficult. One's vision is blurred.

But very quickly, usually in a matter of days, leaders and people alike try to minimize the impact of the loss of a pastor and act as if everything were under control and back to normal. Such is not the case, of course, but on the surface, it looks as if all the bases were covered and the parish would sail right on to the final transition stage of integration. This is an illusion. The leaders and people are heading down the trough toward "the pit." Denial will not stop the slide.

What is needed more than anything else at this stage is not a quick and sudden naming of a new pastor. What is needed is an interval for grieving, letting go, uncertainty and anxious waiting for a new pastor. Easter did not follow immediately after Good Friday. The tomb experience came next. All saw where Jesus was laid and then they withdrew to their own homes. So also with a parish that is in a sudden, unexpected period of transition.

What is needed at this time is a group – a transition team – to shepherd the parish through this difficult time. Ideally, the diocese or other outside resource will provide facilitation to the parish to aid it in the formation and functioning of a transition team during this period. It can also serve as an ideal time for the leaders and people to reflect on what is unique about the parish and what kind of pastor they need to keep the parish moving forward.

The transition team may prepare a report on the parish following the same steps mentioned earlier. The benefits of calling leaders and people together include for the gathering of information and the processing of personal feelings, as well as putting closure to the sudden leave-taking of the pastor. Only then will the parish be able to open its arms to a new pastor. Such a period of corporate and personal reflection does a service not only to the parishioners but to the new person as well. It is to be hoped that the diocese will see the wisdom in not rushing in with a permanent replacement but will take care of immediate sacramental and ministerial needs with temporary supply help. This will give people time to let go of one person before having to open up to another.

Going It Alone in the Interim

The pastor said good-bye, packed his bags and left. It was a grand and fitting farewell, and now he is gone. The empty presider's chair with the open suitcase on it is proof that there is no one to take his place as yet. The interim priests come each weekend to preside at the Masses, but they are not the pastor. The people know that. The ministries continue as before. The staff has its weekly meeting, the council and commissions meet once a month as usual. There is, however, a vacuum, an emptiness that is evident to all who attend the meetings. The weekday services are led by the deacons and staff members. Funerals are handled by neighboring pastors who fill in as needed. Weddings are witnessed by visiting priests. It is a strange period of waiting. Everything continues as before but something is missing. The parish needs a pastor, not only to give it direction but to give it legitimacy and meaning, to set the tone and to affirm it on its journey. "Will anyone apply?" the people ask. "Does anyone want to join us on the journey? Are we a threat or do we have a bad reputation? What will become of us?"

Such questions are typical of a parish in the interim period between pastors. It is a time of unknowing, of chaos. It is the pits. But it also leads to new insight and growth. Parishioners begin to realize that they do have something to offer, that theirs is a good parish, that they have much going for themselves as a community of believers. Given the right pastor they can really go somewhere.

Close communication between the transition team and the diocese is most important during this period. We realize, however, that this may not be possible in all dioceses. In the ideal situation, the team provides weekly updates and bulletins to the leadership and parishioners about the process of selecting a replacement. How many priests (or pastoral administrators) saw the parish report. When the placements are likely to be named. How long it will be after the pastor is named before the person arrives. Without pushing or making a pest of itself, the transition team must keep in close touch with the diocesan contact people, assuring them respect and appreciation for their difficult task of finding a suitable person, but also emphasizing that secrecy and noncommunication can have a detrimental effect on their work.

At last a person is named. The news spreads quickly. Stories abound about the person's history, likes and dislikes, quirks and assets, most not grounded in fact. Ideally, the new pastor will not arrive immediately but will take a break from his previous assignment. This also allows time for the stories to die down and to let truth prevail. This interim gives the leaders and the transition team time to prepare for the welcoming of the new pastor and a chance to reflect on what they have to offer the new person. This is an especially anxious time for the pastoral staff. Will they keep their jobs? Will they be able to fit in with the style and tone of the new pastor? One of the tasks of the team is to minister to the staff, helping staff members process their fears and anxieties in the interim period.

Welcoming the New Pastor

The final task of the transition team is to provide a welcoming environment for the new pastor. One parish, the first weekend that the new pastor was in the parish, had him preside at all the Masses. He walked up the aisle to the presider's chair, took the stole that was laid over the open suitcase, put it on, closed the suitcase, handed it to the transition team and then announced to the congregation, "Greetings. I'm your new pastor." The place erupted with spontaneous applause at every Mass.

The insights of chapter 6, of course, apply to this situation. Neither the new pastor nor the transition team has the advantage of sharing insights with other new pastors or teams going through the same process. It must be done "in-house." One task of the team is to provide feedback and insight to the new pastor a few months into the pastorate. This is best done at a special session between pastor and team, perhaps facilitated by diocesan personnel or an outside facilitator. This is the time to share impressions of the first few months of the "new dispensation" and to assess hints and hunches about future directions.

If there is obvious unrest and friction between the pastor and significant groups or individuals in the parish, this is the time to locate the sources of the conflict and take steps to foster dialogue and mutual understanding between the opposing parties. Glossing over the difficulties or pretending they don't exist does a disservice to the pastor and fosters unrest among the leaders and people. Having an objective facilitator from outside the situation helps bring the issues to the surface and offers hope for insight and perhaps a resolution of the conflict.

By Thanksgiving all the pieces are in place for the new pastorate. The parish is starting out on a new journey with new leadership. The tasks of the transition team are almost over. Soon it will be time for its members to put closure to their work and return to their original ministries and positions in the parish. The pastor, staff and council can take it from here.

The team has one last duty to perform, one that is of service to the larger Church more than to the parish. The year-long process of transition has had its ups and downs. Some things worked well and others could have been better. The parish and the team itself learned much from the experience. This knowledge and insight should not be lost. It needs to be shared with the diocese and with other parishes who may soon be undergoing a change of pastors.

Because of all the wisdom gained during the process, the transition team needs to write up a description of its experience and submit it to the bishop and diocesan personnel. This report should include a detailed description of the process and an analysis of what worked and didn't work over the year, along with recommendations of how the diocese might use this in other parishes. It may, of course, fall on deaf ears and nothing may come of it, but at least the team shared its experience and provided a model of how much can be gained through careful attention to the stages and steps of transition. As more and more parishes participate in the process and offer their insights to the larger Church, eventually a new tradition will be born, one that is more inclusive and involving of parish leaders and people and is more rewarding for the pastors themselves.

Parishes Run by Religious Congregations

Not all parishes are run by the diocese. Some are staffed by religious congregations of men, each with its own charism and style of operation. The placement of pastors in these parishes is under the jurisdiction of the provincial or regional headquarters of the congregation. While working with some of these parishes, we have often heard the complaint that pastors are changed too often and with little or no consultation with parish leaders or parishioners. "Just as we get to know one pastor and begin to understand his style of leading and his vision for the parish," one person remarked, "he is pulled out suddenly and we have to start all over with a new person."

Rarely is much consideration given to the parish community and its involvement in the transition of religious order pastors. As long as the charism and identity of the congregation stays intact, the provincial leadership reasons, nothing more is needed to provide for continuity through the transition from one pastor to another. So many opportunities, however, for growth and insight are lost, both by the congregation and by the parish itself. Many options for the creative use of the transition period exist if people are given the chance to reflect on the change and to offer suggestions.

We were recently called to help facilitate the transition of a number of parishes staffed by a religious order that were in close proximity. Five pastors would be leaving, replaced by only three priests that would serve the five parishes. The provincial office had already made the appointments that were to take effect in three months. These new appointments were unknown to the parishioners. Nor were they aware that the number of priests would be reduced from five to three. The local superior of the area called us in to help break the news to parish leaders and to aid them in the transition. This was not an ideal place to begin the process, but one plays the hand one is dealt.

Each of the five parishes sent a contingent of staff and pastoral council members to a full-day conference. The mood was upbeat and positive. They were all aware of a change about to take place and were happy that, for the first time, they were included in the deliberations.

We began by explaining the stages of transition (chap. 2) and laid out the plan the province had for the region. To our surprise, the leaders accepted the proposal with positive reactions. They were relieved to learn that their own parish would not be closed but that they would be served by a team of priests rather than by a resident pastor. They saw this as the order affirming them as a parish and as a sign of new life and resurrection. The transition would not be easy, but death had been averted.

Our next step was to work with the leadership from the five parishes in setting up a transition process for the next six months. Each parish discussed how it would construct a transition team – who would be its members and what would be its duties and responsibilities. The local superior agreed to be the contact and liaison between the parishes and the provincial office.

Clearing up misinformation and ambiguities came next. There had been many rumors and stories circulating in the parishes that had to be corrected. The superior explained in detail when the present pastors would leave, who the members of the new pastoral team would be, the background and experience of each one and when the team would be in place. The parish leaders were relieved to hear, straight from those in authority, what would happen and when. They immediately made plans for disseminating this information to the parishioners. One of the tasks of the newly formed transition teams was to see that everyone got the information and had a chance to discuss its implications in the parish. The teams were also mandated to construct a report from each parish that elaborated their unique character and clientele, as well as the areas they held in common with the other four parishes. These reports would be given to the members of the new pastoral team before they arrived so they might be better prepared for their ministry.

It became obvious during the day that the parish staffs were anxious about the transition. They were not sure that their jobs would continue if the parishes would be served by a team of priests. The regional superior tried to allay their fears by assuring them that their services would be needed all the more so with two fewer priests. He also agreed, with our urging, to have a special session with all the staff members from the five parishes and the three new priests within the next month, long *before* the change would take place. This special meeting would also foster more cooperation between the staffs of the five parishes and begin them on the road to more collaboration and teamwork.

We also urged the province to provide for an interim period after the current pastors left and before the new team was in place. The transition teams would plan ceremonies of departure for the outgoing pastors and would explain the new configuration for pastoring the parishes. The transition teams would also support the parishioners through the interval of letting go of their current pastor and preparing them for the new pastoral team. On its part, the province promised to supply temporary priests to the parishes for the month of July. At the end of the month the new team would arrive at a special gathering of all five parish communities for their installation. Over the next few months the parishes and priests would spend time getting to know each other while the transition teams agreed to keep their ears to the ground about how the parishioners were responding to the new setup.

The local superior, who himself would be replaced, committed the province to a second gathering of staffs, councils and transition teams, along with the new team of priests, in November, using outside facilitators in order to assure the success of the project thus far and to plan for the future.

The participants left this initial session with a new sense of ownership in the transition process and with high hopes for the future life and operation of their parishes. What looked like doom and gloom at the beginning of the day turned out to be full of life and new hope at day's end. Many tasks lay ahead from April to November, and many changes would be taking place during that time, but people could see the merits of the new plan and conceded that it might even be an improvement over the present situation. At least the parishes would remain in operation and they might even benefit from greater cooperation among the five communities.

This is but one of many scenarios that could be used with parishes run by religious congregations. All the materials and suggestions contained in this book that address the diocesan situation can apply to religious order parishes as well. What is needed is a change of procedure and the willingness to include parishioners in the process of transition. Most people realize that a province does not have a large pool to draw from in appointing pastors, but they would like a chance to enter into the dialogue.

We worked with another parish staffed by a religious order where there was friction between the priest and people. We gathered the leadership together for a special session of dialogue and feedback. At the end of the session we felt that both the priest and people were understanding each other better and that progress toward a good working relationship was being made. Unfortunately, the pastor did not feel this way and decided to leave the parish the very next day.

The reaction from the religious order was to appoint a new pastor immediately, but we urged them not to do this. The province agreed to have a cooling off period and a time for healing. During this interim several men were approached about becoming the new pastor. Each was encouraged to visit the parish and to talk with the leadership to see if the parish fit their style and expertise. They then reported the experience to the province. Eventually a new pastor was selected, a person who was a good match for the particular needs of the parish.

The parish leaders realized that they were not "interviewing" candidates for the opening, but they did feel respected and valued by the order for their wisdom and insight. Through the experience the province came to understand that when more thought and effort are put into the transition period, the new person is more likely to be successful and thus the province will have fewer headaches later on. The parish came to believe that the province was sensitive to their needs and was willing to include them in the process. As a result, they were more accepting of the new pastor and felt affirmed by the provincial leadership.

Other Parish Transitions

Not only does the pastor change, so do staff and key leaders of the parish. In working with parishes we have found that 54 percent of parish staffs change every three years. In some parishes, the entire membership of the pastoral council changes every three years. In others, half are replaced each year. Transition in parish leadership is the norm, not the exception.

These changes, however, do not have the same impact on the direction and tone of the parish that a change in pastor does. Nevertheless, they do need to be given attention commensurate with the position. A change of school principal, for instance, can change the tone of the school, which in turn changes the morale of teachers, which affects the students' response, which is felt by parents and eventually the parish as a whole.

The search process for filling staff positions is more uniform and better developed than for changing in pastors. For one thing, the parish itself has more control over the process. A search committee seeks out qualified people and makes recommendations to the appropriate body or to the pastor for eventual placement. Nevertheless, the materials used in this book can be adapted to fit transitions of staff members and council personnel.

Suppose a music minister who has served the parish for many years is retiring and a replacement must be found. The pastoral council, with the pastor, begins the process by naming a small transition team. The team can be the liturgy committee itself. More than likely, however, only one or two of the liturgy committee will be members of the team, along with a member of the staff, perhaps a choir member, a leader of song and a parishioner-at-large. The team has the following responsibilities:

- To gather data from the choir, the leaders of song, the guitar group, a sampling of parishioners that allows the music minister to recognize the gift he or she has been to the parish.
- To reflect on how the parish has, in return, been gift to the person.
- To translate this information into answers to the questions: To whom do we need to say special thank-you's and good-bye's? What fences, if any, need to be mended?
- To plan, with key music people, the farewell party.
- To gather information from choir members, leaders of song and Mass-goers their ideas for the future, including what they hope to maintain, what they would like to discontinue and what they would like to see introduced.
- Using this information, the team develops a profile of the music needs in the parish, as well as the desires of the worshiping community and those responsible for directing and leading the music.
- To be involved, along with others, in the interviewing of candidates.
- To assure an orientation process for the newly hired music minister.
- To plan a welcome ritual and celebration.

The same approach can be used for any staff member. The key to success is the care taken in naming the transition team, preparing it for its task and supporting it during the process. Planning an interim period between placements also helps people adjust to the changes.

One parish, for example, after searching for a director of religious education and interviewing a number of candidates, decided to have a one-year interim period during which the members of the education commission coordinated the program with the help of two seasoned religious education secretaries. During the interim, parents of students and other qualified parishioners came forward, not only to teach but to help manage the overall program as well. It worked so well that the commission began to wonder whether this was not a better situation than having a paid staff position.

In the end, they did hire a new person, primarily for the expertise and background experience she could afford the program. The new coordinator was highly qualified and accepted the position because the people were so cooperative and ready to work *with* her in providing quality education and formation for all ages in the parish.

The same guidelines can be followed for a change of principals, taking into account the policies of the diocesan school board with regard to hiring. In most situations, a parish school board or an education commission is already in place. This group has the responsibility for hiring the new principal, with the cooperation and approval of the pastor. Instead of a transition team being appointed, the school board may function in this capacity. On the other hand, the school board or education committee might appoint a transition team made up of board members, teachers, staff and parents. This team could be helpful to the principal who is leaving the parish and to the new person taking the position. Perhaps the team's most significant contribution is the development of a profile of the school community. This profile is the result of consultations with faculty, parents, board members and staff. This team is in an excellent position to bring a fresh approach as well as objectivity to the task because they would not be involved in the history of the school to the same extent as the school board or education commission. The school profile could be used by the board to advertise the position and could also be shared with potential candidates.

As for the replacement of pastoral council members and other key parish leadership positions, one parish had a permanent transition committee in place that shepherded the leaders through the changes each year. It was up to this group to call a gathering of all the ministers of the parish each year out of which the new commission members were selected. The transition committee arranged for each commission to nominate people who would serve on the pastoral council for the next two years. From these nominees, lots were drawn at the weekend Masses that would decide who the new council members would be. This committee also helped the council and commissions through a discernment process for the selection of their chairpersons each year. It became an invaluable group in the parish, one that was specialized in helping the leadership cope with ongoing transition in a creative and caring manner. The transition committee used as its motto the words of St. Paul in the eighth chapter of the letter to the Romans, "The whole of creation is on tiptoe to see the wonderful sight of the sons and daughters of God coming into their own." (Adapted from the J. B. Phillips, *The New Testament in Modern English* New York: Macmillan 1962].)

Changing Leadership in Religious Communities

Since the process of renewal in religious congregations began in the 1970s, more and more communities have turned to some form of discernment in place of a traditional election process. Such an approach usually involves an election committee made up of community members and a facilitator from outside the community. What can the transitioning model offered in this book add to what is already in place?

One of the aspects of discernment that is often missed, both by the person or group leaving office and the community at large, is the need to say an adequate good-bye to one another. Remember the maxim: If you don't say good-bye, you can't say hello! This is especially true in religious communities. If there is not a genuine opportunity to say good-bye to all that was good and graced, as well as all that was painful and difficult, in one administration, the community members are not ready or capable of welcoming the new administration. The result of not saying good-bye is obvious. Community members carry hurts from one administration to the other or compare the new with the former, especially if the members are not pleased with the new approach.

The use of a transition team during a change of administration helps develop creative ways for providing what is needed. Before the installation of the new leadership, for instance, there may be an "out-stallation" for those leaving office. Those who are leaving can be helped to look back, in the light of the community goals, and identify those aspects they feel good about, those the community can be proud of, those they need to ask forgiveness for and those that were not brought to fruition. This information can be shared with the community in a prayer ritual. It may include a "state-of-the-community" reflection followed by a formal leave-taking. It can be something as simple as a greeting of peace or an individual blessing given to each member of the community by the person or group leaving office. Adequate time should be given, either during this ritual or in private, for any reconciliation that needs to be voiced to the outgoing administration. A party, of course, follows the prayer ritual.

How the other components of the model described in the book can be divided between the chapter or the election committee of the congregation and the transition team varies with each community. What is important is to make sure they are all addressed, including a possible interim period between administrations to allow the community to let go of one style of leadership and embrace the new.

We have included at the end of this chapter a process for the discernment of new leadership in religious communities. It is offered as a further resource for a successful transition of administrations in religious congregations. With adaptations, it can be utilized with other groups as well.

Yes, We Can Do It on Our Own!

Throughout this chapter we have been applying the general principles of transition to individual parishes and other situations. Of course, the ideal is to have a transition process established in a diocese or religious congregation as a whole, so that there is a common experience to draw upon. Everyone knows what to expect and "how we do things around here." Priests and people know what is expected of them, when the placement will be made and how the process works. Surprises and secrecy are kept to a minimum.

This is the ideal. The American Catholic Church has not reached that point in its history. Hopefully, a few dioceses and religious congregations will take the risk and establish a comprehensive, year-long process for the change of pastors. Most parishes, however, are not part of these few dioceses. They must do it on their own and act as models and prophets to the diocese and to other parishes in their vicinity.

Our hope is that some parishes will take us up on the offer and inaugurate a well-planned, comprehensive process of transition when they know that their pastor will be leaving the parish. One advantage for doing this is that there will be a better chance the new pastor will be aware of what the parish is like and will come ready to fit into the tradition and uniqueness of the parish. It is well worth spending this time on the transition process because the ramifications of the outcome will last for years to come.

Discerning Community Leadership

Discernment is not magic. It is not something that can be "turned on" when needed. The gift of discernment flows from a life stance of reflective prayer. To the degree that one allows the Word of God to influence the events of daily life, one is learning to discern.

Communal discernment is an experience of group reflection on the Word. It is the effort of each member of the community to hear the Word that is spoken in and through the lives and wisdom of one another. It is hearing the Word, respecting it and treasuring it as the wisdom the Spirit gives to the group at any given time. A community must want to discern. It must decide together that this is important. To do this intelligently, community members need an understanding of the philosophy of shared wisdom. This is the first step toward the decision to discern new leadership.

The philosophy of shared wisdom includes an understanding of the promise of Jesus to be with us always. In the Gospel of Matthew, Jesus promises that whenever we come together he will be with us (Mt. 18:20). He explains how this will happen in the promise that his Spirit will be with us always. What Jesus does in the Gospel of Matthew is to assure us that we each receive a piece of the wisdom. No one gets it all (except God, of course!) and we each get different pieces. These pieces come out of our lived experiences. To the degree that we are willing to process our daily lives and reflect on the events of each day, then we are able to name and claim our piece of the wisdom. To the degree that we are willing to share our piece of wisdom and listen, reverently and trustingly, to all the other pieces, to that degree we are in a discerning mode as a community.

Discernment calls for a commitment to a process that demands time, energy, honesty and personal vulnerability. There is a discipline that is required in this commitment, as well as a spirit of self-sacrifice and penance. It is not only an individual commitment to speak one's truth, but a corporate responsibility to speak, to hear and to synthesize all the wisdom available in the group. Community members must see it as a journey they will take together. They must be committed to support one another on that journey and to accept the outcome gracefully.

A number of attitudes and circumstances can block the ability of a community to discern. These need to be named and faced. One of the blocks occurs when a community follows certain procedures that are *called* discernment but are not, in fact, genuine experiences of discernment. Another block is when a community has done a partial discernment but has chosen not to follow the process to completion. They think they have discerned and that it hasn't worked, so they want no more of it. Such groups need help to identify past experiences of discernment so as to determine what they would need to change if they are to give validity to the process.

Another block can be the result of frequent use. There are communities who have used a discernment process many times and have begun to question the time commitment involved. The temptation is to shorten the process. It is not possible, however, to nurture the necessary climate and arrive at a discerned decision without adequate time for prayer, listening and group sharing.

Some community members have difficulty understanding the importance of doing more than just praying for the guidance of the Spirit. It is important to recall that God has gifted us with both intellects and emotions. We are capable of gathering information, analyzing and synthesizing the results and making reasonable choices. We are also capable of intuitive feelings that allow subjective reality to influence objective truth. We are called during the discernment process to make use of our gifts of mind and soul, to bring both our heads and our hearts to the process, to use critical judgment and lived experience. It is in *all* human reality that the Spirit lives and speaks.

While there is no one way to discern, there are certain attitudes and behaviors that are critical to the process. Trust is essential. People must trust themselves and their personal wisdom, they must trust each other and they must trust the Spirit to be at work in the gathering.

Holy indifference is another critical attitude. This is a very difficult stance, but it is absolutely necessary if the Spirit is to be free to function within the group. Each person must approach the process completely open to all possibilities. To decide in advance whom you will vote for or whom you will not vote for is to interfere with the work of the Spirit. The community needs to recognize attitudes and behaviors that are sins against the Spirit. These include a refusal to cooperate with the process, an attitude of distrust, an effort to influence another's opinion or decision and predeciding choices before starting the process.

The question is often asked, "How can we nurture a spirit of holy indifference in the group as a part of our communal preparation for discernment?" Two activities come to mind. Revisiting the community's history and retelling the stories of bygone years are powerful means toward recognizing the action of the Spirit. It becomes clear that God's strength is present in human weakness. God becomes visible in human vulnerability. If adequate time is given to reflecting on the past and to learning from the group's history, it helps the members to trust that God continues to walk the journey with them.

Another preparation for communal discernment is to engage the community in faith-sharing experiences. This allows the members to explore their own faith journey and to share with each other experiences of letting go and letting God act in their lives.

If discernment is to happen, the community must also trust the facilitator of the process. It is important that they have some experience of working with the facilitator before entering into the discernment process. It is advisable to have the facilitator do an orientation with the community months prior to the discernment as a means of becoming acquainted and comfortable with each other. If the "match" is not right, the process will be hampered.

Discernment is holy work. It is also hard work. Informed commitment is required on the part of each community member, as well as a willingness to learn how to discern and to allow time for the Spirit to touch the lives and hearts of all those involved in the process. Haste prevents an authentic discernment. Discernment, first and foremost, demands that a group surrender to holy leisure.

To make a community decision through discernment calls for a deep personal faith and a willingness on the part of each person to let go of the need to control, to win, or always to be right. This call to faith is threefold:

1. I must have faith in my own ability to allow the Spirit to reach and touch me and faith in my own wisdom so

that I can speak it. I also must have faith in the wisdom of others so that I can hear, respect and treasure it.

2. I must have faith in the other members of the group that they, too, are trying to hear and speak their own wisdom as it is given them by the Spirit. And that they are sincere in listening to my wisdom.

3. I must have faith in the Spirit that, in fact, it is the wisdom of God being shared in the gathering. I must believe that the Spirit desires to guide us and will do this if we allow it to happen.

This, in other words, is a prayerful, reflective, faith-filled process, not a political exercise! There are four practical expectations built into the discernment design:

1. The persons chosen for leadership must know what the community expects of them. Critical to the process is the community's willingness to agree upon a common direction and goals for itself. The leaders also need to know how they are perceived by the community in terms of strengths, limitations and needs.

2. The community needs to hear how the future leaders perceive their own gifts and limitations in the light of community goals and how invested they are in these goals.

3. The community must look at what it calls *itself* to as it calls some of its members to leadership roles. Too often the burden of accomplishing future directions, as well as the mandate to listen, to serve, to love, to model and to challenge has been given solely to the leaders. The mutuality of responsibility must be both considered and embraced and then translated into the expectations the community has for itself.

4. A discernment process will not solve the problems of a community. Nor should it be used for that purpose. No community is perfect. There will always be some degree of fear and mistrust, some lack of clarity about its mission, some disunity, some dysfunctional behaviors and some controlling members. If any of these, or

other issues like them, are preventing the group from moving forward, identifying new leadership will not provide a solution. The facilitator must have the courage to name the problem and the community must be willing to deal with the issues if discernment is to succeed. Only then can the process do what it is designed to do: identify leadership.

The Process of Discerning New Leadership

The amount of time required for each step of the process depends on many variables. The total discernment of new leadership requires four to five complete days.

Step 1: Input on the philosophy of shared wisdom and discernment
Reflection
Discussion of implications
Overview of design, questions and concerns

Step 2: Review of community's goals and directions

Step 3: Theological reflection on leadership and authority

Step 4: Identification of qualities, experience and skills needed to lead the community at this time, given the agreed upon direction and goals. This is done with the understanding that no one person will possess all the qualities needed.

Step 5: The concept of mutuality is introduced. For each quality expected of the new leader, the group names what the community will expect of itself. Time is then given for prayerful reflection and discussion on what has surfaced.

Step 6: Identification of those with leadership potential

   A. Time is given for prayerful consideration of people with some of the qualities listed. Each person is encouraged to think of three or four names and the reasons those names come to mind.

B. Initial recommendations are made. Anyone who so desires makes a recommendation to the assembly by saying: *I wish to have us consider (name) because . . .*

Names and reasons are recorded on newsprint. While there is a limit on the number who can be considered, a few words of caution are in order. This is not a popularity contest. Nor is it a time to affirm people in order to make them feel accepted. Recall again that discernment should not be used to solve problems or heal people.

If the community is larger than thirty or forty members, this surfacing of names works best if it is done in smaller groups of ten to twelve. Each smaller group records names of candidates and reasons for their choices. This information is written on newsprint and displayed where all can see it. Time is given for everyone to walk around, in silence, and read what all the groups have recorded.

C. The initial discussion of candidates takes place in table groups. The focus is on questions such as, Were there any surprises for you in the names that surfaced? Did you learn anything new about the persons identified?

D. An extended period of quiet is then provided for personal prayer. Each person is asked to write down their top three choices, in priority order. This first consensus test will provide an indication as to where the Spirit is leading the group.

E. The facilitator tabulates the choices and presents them to the community without revealing the names. Each candidate is given a number and the people see that number one received so many votes, number two received so many votes, and so forth. This information is studied and

then, based purely on the way the choices fall
and without knowing the names, the community decides how many will be asked to remain
in the process.

F. The facilitator then presents the names to the
group in alphabetical order, not in the order of
choice.

G. When can a person withdraw? Ideally, all those
asked to remain in the process will do so. It is
important that they hear the call of the community. Circumstances, however, may make that
impossible. Anyone who feels the need to withdraw dialogues first with the facilitator and then
with the community before doing so.

Step 7: A guided reflection on listening with the ear of the
heart begins this step.

A. The strengths of each potential leader are now
considered.
Anyone who wishes to speak, does so by saying:
*If (name) is discerned as our leader, it will be good
for the community because . . .*

B. After the strengths of each candidate have been
considered, the next step is to identify limitations, needs or concerns. Again, anyone who
wishes to speak does so by saying:
If (name) is discerned, the risk will be . . .
or:
If (name) is discerned, the needs will be . . .
or:
If (name) is discerned, my concern would be . . .

C. The potential leaders now have time to reflect
on their strengths and limitations and to prepare their responses. They will share with the
community their own perception of their gifts
and limitations and will tell the community what
they, as leaders of the community, would expect

of the members. Questions may be asked and discussion follows.

D. After a period of prayer, a consensus test is taken with everyone choosing just one person. Before the results of this initial consensus test are reported by the facilitator, it is appropriate to do a reflection on holy indifference. This is the "letting go" time in the process. The results of this consensus will indicate where the Spirit is taking the group. The personal grace needed is the willingness to move from the "I" to the "we." No longer is it what *I* think is best but rather what are *we* saying as a community.

E. The result of this consensus test will determine what happens next. There may be a need to talk more at the individual tables. Additional questions to the potential leaders may be needed. Time for prayer may be requested. Whatever is done, the goal is to reach as near a consensus as possible before moving on to the next step.

Step 8: After a period of private reflection, each member of the community is asked to fill out the following form:

As I am hearing the Spirit, I believe we should call (name) to be our next leader because:

The results of this private reflection are turned in to the facilitator who will be the only person to see them. They are not signed.

In the context of prayer, these are read out loud by the facilitator as community members listen with their hearts. This completes the process of discernment. There only remains the affirmation of the discernment through the canonical vote.

Chapter Eight

Wisdom for the Journey

Transitions never happen as planned. The house always takes longer to build than expected, it costs more than predicted and it never turns out according to the blueprints. So, too, with our proposed process of transition. Adaptations and changes happened at every stage. This chapter highlights what the experience has taught us and can serve as a checklist for success in applying the process to each unique situation.

Council Appoints the Team

Creating a parish transition team is an essential component of a successful transition process. This is the group that directs and guides the parish through the changes. Originally we thought the pastor would be the best person to appoint people to this team, using the guidelines for membership mentioned in chapter 3. After listening to feedback from the parishes involved in the pilot project, we now feel that the pastoral council is the best body to do the selection of the team. The outgoing pastor, of course, is a member of the pastoral council and, therefore, is involved in the selection. But letting the council do this task gives the members more ownership in the transition process. This tells the parishioners that the team is not a select group of the pastor's friends and confidants. It also gives the council more authority in holding the team accountable throughout the transition and in maintaining the council's oversight role in the parish. The council can support and aid the team if and when it gets bogged down or encounters difficulty. One team, for example, appointed the staff person as chair of the group, even though the guidelines suggested some-one other than a staff member be the leader. The result was that the team tended to acquiesce in favor of the staff person and not carry an equal share of the workload. This would be one place where the council might step in and suggest that a new chair be appointed. The outgoing pastor may not be able or willing to make this intervention because he may be preoccupied with his own leave-taking or may not be aware of the difficulty.

Special Staff Session

A second piece of wisdom learned in the process was that the parish staffs need time to process the impact of a change in pastors and to air feelings about how the transition will affect them personally. They are the ones who will experi-ence the change in tone and direction to the greatest extent. They have the most to lose in the transition. Their very jobs and livelihoods are at stake.

Our suggestion is that in the first phase of the process, when outgoing pastors gather for mutual support and in-sight, so too should the parish staffs. They need a chance to gather as a group with other staffs to talk about their expe-rience of the current pastorate and to discuss fears and concerns about letting go of the present pastor and accept-ing the new.

The session lasts three to four hours. This time is well spent in preparing the staff for the shift in leadership. The gathering happens in January or February, at the same time or shortly after the sessions for outgoing pastors and the transition teams. The content of the meeting includes an explanation of the transition process and its predictable steps. It also includes time for staff members to clarify issues of tenure and job security, letting go of set ways of operating and identifying traditions established during the current pastorate. They are also be encouraged to open up to new ways of doing things, as well as working through "what if" scenarios. Some of these scenarios may include "what if" a new pastor is not appointed immediately and the staff has to operate without a resident pastor for an extended period of time. "What if" the new pastor is the exact opposite of the present one and has a different understanding of the staff's role in the parish? "What if" no priest is available for the opening and a nonordained administrator is appointed? These, and many others, can be the occasion not only for a lively discussion but for preparing the staffs for possible changes resulting from the transition.

This is not the only time the staff will be discussing issues related to the change in pastors. One of the initial tasks of the transition team will be to meet with the staff and pastoral council, either in a joint session or separately, as a first step in gathering information for the parish report. The staff will give its insights into what the parish needs to hold on to, what it needs to let go of and what new things it should try out. Staff members will also be asked to act as facilitators for the parish town hall sessions.

This preliminary session with staffs undergoing transition is different. It provides a safe setting among one's peers to get in touch with unspoken, and perhaps up to this point unknown, concerns, fears and issues related to the change.

Depending on the circumstances, it may also be helpful to have a second gathering of staffs in the fall after the new pastor has been appointed and has been in place for a few months. This mutual interchange of staffs from various parishes undergoing the "new beginning" can be a support and a time for new insight into what the new pastorate might mean for those who are the professional ministers in the parish. Care must be taken in describing the purpose of this gathering so that the new pastors do not perceive the meeting as staff talking behind their backs or as a time for airing gripes and longing for "the good old days." If it can be done in a positive context and as one more help in fostering a good transition process, then it can serve as an asset to the future life, not only of the parish but to the vitality of staff itself.

The positioning of this fall gathering of staffs should happen either before or within the same week as the gathering of new pastors and the transition teams. The insights gleaned from the staff session are helpful to share with the pastors and teams at their final session together.

Later Meeting for Prospective Pastors

In the original design we held three series of workshops, one in January, one in June and one in October or November. The first and second series included workshops for outgoing pastors, transition teams and prospective pastors. The third series was for the new pastors and the transition teams.

One of the diocesan committees suggested that having the prospective pastors meet in January was too early. Those looking for a new pastorate were either unsure about making a change or were unwilling to commit themselves for fear that the people they now serve would get nervous about a possible change.

Much as we tried to encourage dioceses and priests to be open about transitions and to prepare early for changes, there was some reluctance by the priests to do this. The result was that in some of the parishes involved in the pilot project, the new pastors had not attended the prospective pastors' workshops. They were appointed from a pool of possible candidates outside the process. One new pastor, who experienced the benefits of the final session in the fall of the year, expressed sadness in not being part of the previous two workshops. He could have gained so much, he said, from the preparation and insight provided to prospective pastors. It was evident to him that those who had attended all three prospective pastors' sessions were better prepared and ready for the change.

To overcome this reluctance to commit to the prospective pastors' workshop, one alternative is to hold the first session for prospective pastors later in the spring rather than in January. In this new schedule, the outgoing pastors and the transition teams still have their workshops in January.

The parish staffs may also have a gathering at this time. The transition teams then go to work preparing a parish report and profile for the diocese. The deadline for completion is the middle of April. By the first of May these parish reports are available for distribution to prospective pastors and pastoral administrators.

According to this plan, the best time for hosting a gathering of prospective pastors is the end of April or the beginning of May. At this session, the prospective pastors not only have the opportunity to discuss what they will have to let go of in choosing a new position but also receive the reports of places they may consider as a new pastorate. They receive guidance in what to look for in studying the reports and how to discern whether they may be a good fit for a parish, given their inclinations and capabilities.

In the weeks following the prospective pastors' workshop, each person comes to a decision about which parish or parishes to apply for. This request goes to the diocesan personnel board and the local ordinary for selection. The appointment is made by June but the new pastor does not arrive at the parish immediately. There is, instead, an interim period during which the parish is able to let go of the outgoing pastor and start looking forward to the new replacement. This also gives the new appointee a break between assignments for updating, vacation and adjustment. The newly appointed pastors gather in June for mutual support and insight during the "in-between" period. This is a critical moment for reflecting on past successes and failures, and for preparing for the new pastorate.

The exact timing for the prospective pastors' workshops will vary in each diocese, but the insight is the same. Consider putting off the first workshop for this group until the parish reports are finished and until the priests and pastoral administrators are comfortable making public that they are at least considering a change. Some of those who attended our prospective pastors' workshop in the past knew this might not be the year to request a transfer. Once they saw, however, what was involved in the process, their intentions changed. They decided that, yes, this would be a good time to move. Situating this first workshop in late April or early May, and having parish reports available for consideration, can provide the right moment and the necessary information for priests and administrators to consider changing their place of ministry. That is not to say that prospective pastors be kept in the dark about diocesan intentions for their placement. We encourage the personnel board to invite prospective pastors to consider a move early in the year and to provide information to priests and administrators about possible openings and options. What we are suggesting is a more productive workshop for prospective pastors. This might happen if it is held a few months after the ones for outgoing pastors, transition teams and parish staffs.

Parish-Based Workshops for Teams

One of the dioceses involved in the pilot was a smaller, more rural diocese where the parishes were spread over a large geographical area. It was difficult for the transition teams to gather in one place, especially during the winter months. As an adjustment to their situation, we held the team sessions all on one night, starting at 5 p.m. and lasting until 10 p.m. This was not easy for team members, but they made the sacrifice to be there because they found it a worthwhile contribution to their parish. What was lost in this arrangement was the personal reflection period between the two consecutive evenings of the workshop. What was gained was having to make only one trip instead of two during the week. Once people arrived at the common meeting place, the participants became energized and excited about their task of shepherding the parish through the transition process. Their evaluations showed this. But they also asked for another way of operating that would not require long travel times.

The bishop and the diocesan committee of this rural diocese decided to continue using this new approach to transition, but they felt some adaptation was necessary. What they planned to do was continue with a joint gathering of outgoing pastors led by a professional facilitator, as well as one for prospective pastors. But for the transition teams, the diocese decided to train a core group of facilitators drawn from parish staffs and lay leaders who would conduct workshops for the transition teams in each parish. No longer would the teams come together for a common meeting. Instead, the trained facilitators would go from parish to parish leading the workshops and bringing with them the insights and experiences from other transition teams. What was lost, of course, was the mutual interchange, support and insight provided by a joint gathering of teams. What was gained was a chance to reflect on their unique situation without having to travel to a common location.

The wisdom of this adaptation is the need to remain flexible during the transition process. One model does not fit all. Each diocese and individual parish must decide what best fits their unique situation. What we hope is maintained throughout these adaptations is the importance of the transition period for the life and vitality of a parish. It deserves an ongoing process covering many months and not just a concentrated effort a few weeks before and after the change takes place. As more thought and energy are put into the transition period, fewer problems and anxieties confront a parish in the years following the change of pastors.

Redoing the Appointment

The risk in every pastoral assignment is that the appointment may fail. A new pastor is named, but after a few months it becomes apparent that this is not a good match. This happened during the pilot project. When the transition teams had gathered in the fall of the year after the pastors had been appointed, it was obvious that one team was not in good spirits. The other teams were talking about the joy they experienced in welcoming the pastor and what prospects were on the horizon. This one team, however, felt dejected and disillusioned because of what had happened in the parish since the new person arrived.

This is not to say that all the other teams felt that the Messiah had just been named their pastor, or that there were not rough edges to be smoothed out in the transition. The sentiment of this particular team was altogether different from the others. We sensed that a substantial problem existed with the placement.

The next day we met with the new pastors for their session. We listened to the stories of each new pastor and what had transpired over the first few months of their pastorate. Knowing there are always two sides to every situation, we listened with open minds to the story of the pastor in the parish where the team expressed difficulties. The pastor's explanation was that all was going well. "Only a small group was causing problems and they did not represent the people as a whole." Unfortunately, this new pastor had not been part of any of the previous prospective pastors' workshops, so we had no way of knowing his previous experience or his style of leading. We encouraged him to come to the joint meeting of new pastors and transition teams that evening. He declined the offer, pleading a previous engagement. The other pastors listened intently to his story, all of them having to adjust to new situations as well. They offered suggestions and insights, as well as a strong urgency to change his other commitment in order to come to the joint session. He refused.

That evening the transition teams and new pastors came together for a dinner and a final meeting. While other groups of teams and pastors spent time sharing stories and hints about the future, we, as facilitators, sat with the team that was having difficulties to strategize what to do with their situation. They asked that the diocese intervene and provide help in what appeared to be a bad experience that would only get worse over time. Evidence emerged that the problem was not isolated to a few people but affected the parish as whole.

The next day we met with the diocesan committee to evaluate the entire process. Much time was spent on this particular parish. Should the present pastor remain or should some other arrangement be made? Our concern was that everyone was suffering, the pastors as well as the parish-ioners. It appeared that it might well get worse in the months and years ahead. The meeting ended with a commitment by the personnel board to alert the local vicar of the situation, as well as the bishop.

Many deliberations followed in the next few months and within a short period the pastor announced his decision to leave for another assignment. At the time, it appeared to be a no-win situation. Some of the staff members decided to resign as well. In the long term, however, it was helpful to the parish and to the priest himself. He got the help and guidance he needed. The parish got new leadership that better fit its style and temperament.

In our minds, this one case study is proof that the pilot project was a success. Those involved in the placement were able to discover a mismatch of pastor and people early in a new pastorate. As a result, they were able to make changes before either party experienced serious harm. This is the risk and benefit associated with a year-long process for a change in pastors. We encourage dioceses and religious congregations to pay attention to this reality and when it occurs to make the necessary adjustments before the pastor or the parish community experiences long-lasting harm to body and spirit.

No Priest Available

It can happen in searching for a new pastor that no suitable priest is available to become the pastor for a parish in transition. The temptation is to find a "warm body" and send him in as the pastor. The new person, however, may not be equipped for the job or may not be physically or psychologi-cally up to the task. The diocese of Richmond, Virginia, acknowledged this in a planning document they published in 1989. It stated that not "every priest ordained for the diocese is by virtue of ordination gifted to pastor a parish community in the diocese. The diocese needs to liberate those priests who do not have the gifts for the role of pastor to engage in other forms of ministry" (report from the *Task Force of Future Mission and Ministries*, Diocese of Richmond, 1989, p. 18). Not every doctor is suited for surgery, not every teacher can inspire sophomores, not every lawyer is gifted to conduct trials in court. Why should every priest be able to pastor every parish?

This will become a critical issue as the pool of available candidates for pastoring parishes keeps shrinking. Both dioceses and religious congregations are facing this shortage and are trying to cope with the consequences as well as they can. The temptation is to appoint people who are not good matches for the parish community. Can the process outlined in this book provide insight into this dilemma?

Two cases surfaced during the pilot. One was a temporary solution, the other long-term. In both situations, the parish was losing an ordained pastor who was well-liked by the parishioners. Both results were successful. One place was a large, suburban parish with a capable professional staff. No pastor was available for placement by the interim period of June and July. The outgoing pastor had already left. The other parishes that were part of the transition process of the diocese had some sense of who their new pastor might be or knew that at least a few priests had expressed interest. They felt confident that they would have a pastor by the end of the summer. For the parish in question, no prospective pastor was forthcoming, or even on the horizon. The mood of the transition team was near panic. What would happen to their parish if no pastor were found? We tried to console them and ease their fears. The diocesan committee assured them that a pastor would eventually be found. We also told them not to push the diocese for a rapid replacement. Having a longer interim period would be an asset rather than a hindrance. They swallowed hard and began to cool down, trying to look at the long view and not the short haul, to see the forest and not just the trees. We kept emphasizing the need for a *good* match and not just *any* match.

As a matter of fact, no immediate replacement was found. The parish was given a part-time priest administrator who would serve the parish for only one year. What was in the works, which neither the transition team nor the parish knew about, was the possibility of a priest who was on sabbatical for a year. He was getting a well-earned break and doing some updating. This was the person the diocese felt would be a good pastor for this parish. But the timing was off by one year.

In effect, the parish was undergoing not an interim of a few weeks or months but an interval of one year between pastors. This proved to be very beneficial for all concerned. The parish was given the gift of time to let go of old memories and ways of doing things. The temporary parish administrator had a chance to gain experience in pastoring without long-term worries and concerns. The prospective pastor had a longer period to prepare for the new assignment. Such an arrangement is especially helpful for religious congregations. Many religious were not trained for pastoring parishes. They were involved in teaching, formation or retreat work or chaplaincy. To be assigned to a parish without training and preparation does them a disservice. They need an interim period for updating and preparation. They might also benefit from a year's assignment as temporary administrator to learn the ropes about pastoring a modern parish. Creating a tradition of a longer period of "in-between time" for religious order parishes might provide a service to the parishes and might be an asset to the priests themselves.

The second case of not having an ordained pastor available involved a central city parish with a community of African-American parishioners. The outgoing pastor had served more than his allotted term. It was time for him to change assignments. No priests came forward as candidates to take his place. He continued on as pastor to the end of the summer and still no replacement was available. So he left, wondering what would become of the community. The transition team tried to hold the community together, but people were feeling depressed that no priest "wanted to be their pastor," as they put it. The diocese had been preparing for this eventuality and had been training nonordained pastoral administrators to take on the pastoral duties of a parish where no ordained pastor was available.

Members of the diocesan committee visited the parish and, with the help of the transition team, explained the situation and asked whether the parish would be willing to accept as their pastor someone who was highly qualified but was not a priest. An ordained sacramental minister would also be assigned to the parish to handle the Mass and sacraments. The priest would have other duties as well and would not reside in the parish. The congregation listened intently to the proposal, talked it over among themselves, and they agreed to give it a try.

The new pastoral administrator, an African-American male with much pastoral experience, arrived a week later to the open arms of the people. Sufficient time has now elapsed to evaluate the experiment, and it has worked out well for all concerned. The parishioners have someone who can relate to their experience, even more so than the previous pastor. The priest has an outlet for his pastoral ministry of celebrating Mass with an alive, vibrant community but without other administrative duties. The pastoral administrator has a means for following his vocation of pastoring God's People that he has always felt called to.

The learning from these two cases is that not having a suitable priest pastor available on schedule may not be a drawback. Given the right amount of planning and adaptation, it may prove to be an asset in the long run. The temptation is to make an immediate assignment, no matter who the replacement. Resist this temptation. Work toward a "good" match, even if it takes longer, rather than just "any" match to fill slots.

Adjusted Timeline

Given the corrections and adaptations mentioned above, it is now possible to construct a sample timeline for the transition of pastors. The time at the end of the chapter provides the spacing of events, beginning in September of one year and continuing through November of the next.

The process starts with the diocesan transition committee meeting in September to look over the coming year and to determine which parishes will experience a change of pastors during the course of the year. The committee is led by a director of transition who is freed from other tasks in order to adequately manage this process. Money is allocated from the diocesan budget that is equal to the importance of this task. The members of the committee are also freed from some of their other commitments so they can give this task the time and energy it deserves. The committee will probably not be the same group of people as the diocesan personnel board, although this is a possible option. Our understanding is that the personnel board has other duties to perform, such as placement of associate pastors or apostolic vicars. The personnel board still has the duty, along with the bishop, of appointing pastors. The diocesan committee, on the other hand, includes a wider membership than just priests. Members of this committee not only oversee the transition of pastors but are the liaisons to the parish transition teams as well.

In December, the outgoing pastors and pastoral staffs and councils are notified of the impending change and are given background information about the process they will follow. Parish pastoral councils are also asked to select a transition team using the guidelines mentioned in chapter 3.

In January, three workshops take place. The outgoing pastors assemble for a full day to reflect on their pastorates and to prepare for the change. The transition teams gather on two consecutive evenings, both before and after the pastors' workshop. The parish staffs also have their own half-day session together so they can discuss the implications of the transition.

In February and March, the transition teams start preparing the parish for the change of pastors and assist the pastor in his farewells to the parish. The transition teams sponsor a joint meeting of the staff and council as the first step in constructing a report for the parish. Members of the staff and council act as small group leaders during the parish town hall meetings. The team also designs mailings, transition logos and banners and special leave-taking rituals and gatherings. The diocese contributes information to the parish for inclusion in the report.

By April the transition team will have completed the parish report and profile. At a joint meeting of the staff and council the team presents the report to a diocesan representative, either a member of the diocesan transition committee or someone from the personnel board. The outgoing pastor, staff and council have a chance to nuance, amplify or emphasize aspects of the written report so that diocesan personnel can better understand what it contains.

At the end of April, the prospective pastors gather for their full-day workshop. Not only do they have a chance to discuss with one another why they are looking for a change of assignments but they also can select parish reports that interest them and are given insight into the unique aspects of each parish undergoing change. The diocese may also invite people to this workshop, asking them to consider a change in the near future.

During May, the prospective pastors discern their options and make known to the personnel board the places they feel fit them and why. By the end of the month, the outgoing pastors take leave of the parish. The transition teams, staffs and councils begin their "shepherding" of the parish in the interim period. A temporary "supply" priest fills in during the interval, presiding at Mass and fulfilling other priestly duties.

During June, the second set of workshops takes place. The outgoing pastors have a chance to tell one another what the last six months have been like. When did they hit "the pit"? Have they been able to gain any perspective and start planning for their future? The transition teams gather to gain support from each other and to start planning for the "new reality" that will occur when the pastor arrives. The prospective pastors gather to talk about what may happen when they move into the new place and to work out a "to do" and "not to do" checklist for taking on a new pastorate. This workshop also addresses the disappointments people may feel for not getting their first choice, or any choice at all.

June, or perhaps late May, is also the time the appointments are made by the diocese. This is the ideal time line. Some appointments may not be possible at this time because of the "domino effect." One placement is dependent on another, which is dependent on another, and so forth. Hopefully, however, by planning well in advance for transition, a tradition could be established so that all pastors are named at the same time. This lessens the anxieties of parish leaders and parishioners and gives the pastors a clear expectation of when they will be moving.

In July or August the new pastor arrives in the parish. The transition team prepares for the arrival with ritual and celebrations. The new pastor keeps a log of his first impressions and experiences of the parish, the triumphs and pitfalls. This will serve as material for the next gathering of new pastors.

During September and October, the transition team has a chance to meet with the new pastor and to provide feedback about how the people are responding and to be a conduit for information the pastor may not be able to obtain by other means. The staff, council and parish as a whole grow accustomed to the subtle change in style and tone with the new pastor.

In October or November, the third round of workshops takes place. The transition team meets on the first of two evening sessions to tell their story of welcoming and adjusting to a new pastor. The next afternoon, the new pastors gather to share with one another their story of transition. That evening the pastors and transition teams have a joint session, preceded by a simple meal of celebration. The evening is filled with sharing experiences of change and identifying new emphases and directions for the future.

Sometime during November, the work of the transition team comes to an end. Parish leaders and people have a chance to thank the team for its work and to give them accolades for their hard work and creative ministry. By the end of the year, the new pastor and the parish community are getting used to each other. What was once in turmoil is starting to settle down. What was once in flux and unfrozen is starting to become stabilized and solidified. The parish is looking forward to the next six or more years of leadership from the pastor. The pastor is ready to be "wedded" to the new place. The bishop and diocesan personnel can move on to next year's transitions, knowing that the present batch of pastors and parishes are well suited to each other.

Conclusion

Manufacturers of women's clothing often label garments "one size fits all." Seldom is this so! We do not want to make this claim about the model of transition outlined in this book. However, we do feel there are various components of the model that can be mixed and matched and creatively redesigned by those responsible for making personnel changes in parishes, schools or religious congregations.

There is a great deal of commonality to all transitions. There is a person who is leaving. He or she will need to say good-bye in such a way that the experience is both growthful and hopeful for the one leaving, as well as for those left behind. Those who are leaving can be greatly assisted by a transition group that walks with them on that journey. This same group can also assist those who are responsible for identifying the new replacement. Preparing a profile of those to be served and doing this by gathering the hopes and dreams of those involved is helpful to any search process, as well as to those considering the position.

Transitions are never easy. Mary Anselm Hammerling, O.S.B., speaks powerfully of the transition process in *Discerning Community Leadership* (Ferdinand, Ind.: Immaculate Conception Monastery, 1993).

> Whenever a person is involved with the termination of his or her ministry, some sense of loss and separation is always involved. The experience of loss usually evokes some degree of sadness, pain or loneliness,

even if the possibility of termination arouses hope and excitement in anticipation of new beginnings. The person experiencing the termination, however, does not always realize that those he or she leaves behind, whether an individual, a group, a parish or a community, may also be feeling intense grief and emptiness, for the departure of even one member changes a group. The one leaving and the ones left behind are called to be mutually sensitive to the myriad ambivalent feelings that abound at such times.

This is the pit experience. Loss and grief, however, are only part of the process. From out of the pain comes new insight into who we are and what is essential to our well-being and to our ministry. This leads to new beginnings and an integration of our new selves into the new reality. One transition builds on another so that eventually we discover what is most valuable and essential to our living and to our ministry.

This individual journey is part of the journey of the Church as well. It, too, experiences loss and grief as it lets go of old ways of operating and embraces new realities in a new era. It is our hope that the process of transition offered in this book will aid the Church on this journey of faith.

Bibliography

Times of Transition

Bridges, William. *Transitions: Making Sense of Life's Changes.* New York: Addison-Wesley, 1980.

_____. *Managing Transitions.* New York: Addison-Wesley, 1991.

Dale, Robert D. *Pastoral Leadership.* Nashville: Abingdon, 1986.

DiGiacomo, James J., and John J. Walsh. *So You Want to Do Ministry?* Maryknoll, N.Y.: Orbis Books, 1993.

Forster, Patricia, O.S.F., and Thomas Sweetser, S.J., *Transforming the Parish.* Kansas City, Mo.: Sheed & Ward, 1993.

McKinney, Mary Bennet, O.S.B. *Sharing Wisdom: A Process for Group Discussion Making.* Allen, Tx.: Tabor, 1993.

Mead, Loren B. *Critical Moment of History: A Change of Pastors.* New York: Alban Institute, 1986.

Mitchell, Kenneth, and Herbert Anderson. *All Our Loses, All Our Griefs.* Philadelphia: Westminster, 1993.

Oswald, Roy M., *New Beginnings: A Pastorate Start Up Work Book.* New York: The Alban Institute, 1989.

_____. *Running through The Thistles: Terminating a Ministerial Relationship with a Parish.* New York: The Alban Institute, 1978.

Phillips, William Bud. *Pastoral Transitions.* New York: Alban Institute, 1988.

Rupp, Joyce, O.S.M. *Praying Our Goodbye's.* Notre Dame: Ave Maria, 1988.

Spencer, Sabina, A., and John D. Adams. *Life Changes.* San Luis Obispo, Calif.: Impact Publications, 1990.

White, Edward A. *Saying Goodbye.* New York: Alban Institute, 1990.

Whitehead, James D., and Evelyn E. Whitehead. *Shadows of the Heart.* New York: Crossroad, 1994.

Transition Process: Sample Time Line

Year One		Year Two					
Sept.	Dec.	Jan.	Feb.-Mar.	April	May-June	June 1	June 1-5
Meeting with archdiocesan committee to plan next year's parishes		First round of workshops: 1. Outgoing pastors 2. Transition teams 3. Pastoral staffs from trans. parishes		Prospective pastors receive reports. Special workshop for prospective pastors		Outgoing pastors leave parish	Second set of workshops: 1. Outgoing pastors 2. Trans. teams 3. New pastors
	Outgoing pastors commit to process and appoint transition teams.		Transition teams gather data and present reports to archdiocese.		Prospective pastors make requests and appointments and made.		

June 15-30	July 1 - Oct.	Oct. - Nov.	Nov. - Dec.	[Next Season's Parishes Set]
New pastor arrives in parish after 2-4 week interval	Welcoming of new pastor and feedback by trans team	Third set of workshops 1. New pastors 2. Trans. teams 3. Pastoral staffs	Transition teams have closing ceremony archdiocesan com. evaluation	Start of next year's process in September of year two

About the Authors

Thomas Sweetser, S.J., Ph.D., is co-director of the Parish Evaluation Project, a pastoral consulting group based in Des Plaines, Illinois that teaches parish leaders about methods of successful parish ministry. He is co-author of *Recreating the Parish* and *Transforming the Parish,* both published by Sheed & Ward.

Mary Benet McKinney, O.S.B., D.Min., is a Benedictine Sister from Scholastica Monastery in Chicago. With a background in teaching and administration and her years as staff member at the Chicago Archdiocese School Office, Mary Benet brings a great deal of experience to her consulting work with church systems. Best known for her book *Sharing Wisdom,* she is a national and international lecturer and a practitioner of the art of discernment.